PRAISE FOR *SEVEN MEN*

"This is a book to read, to read aloud to others, and then read again. In a day when children are growing up stunted because of our diet of empty-headed celebrities and contemptible villains, true heroism and manliness needs special nourishment. Eric Metaxas has done it again, and again we are in his debt."

— Os Guinness, author of *A Free People's Suicide*

"One of my favorite authors is Eric Metaxas. His biographies of William Wilberforce and Dietrich Bonhoeffer are compelling and his weekly *Breakpoint* commentaries are powerful and thought provoking. His latest effort, *Seven Men*, is designed to provide men, and those becoming men, with positive role models that practically illustrate what manhood is all about. He does this by focusing on seven men who have lived and served well. We all need great examples; we need to understand what it means to be a man and what God intends men to be; and we need to be inspired. That's what Eric does. I highly recommend this very readable book."

— Denny Rydberg, president of Young Life

"What is true manhood? And what makes a man in our 21st century? These are vital questions that my friend Eric Metaxas helps us wrestle with in this great new book. In looking back to seven outstanding men of history, *Eric helps us understand the essential elements of manhood in any age. This is a superb work—and I highly recommend it.*"

— The Hon. Gregory W. Slayton, author of national bestseller *Be a Better Dad Today*

PRAISE FOR *NEW YORK TIMES* BESTSELLER *BONHOEFFER: PASTOR, MARTYR, PROPHET, SPY*

"This is an important book and I hope many people will read it."

— President George W. Bush

"Eric Metaxas has created a biography of uncommon power—intelligent, moving, well researched, vividly written, and rich in implication for our own lives."

— Archbishop Charles Chaput, *First Things*

"[A] beautifully constructed biography. . . . Throughout his book, but especially toward the end, Metaxas turns this erudite and at times abstruse theologian into a living and tragic human being."

— Alan Wolfe, *New Republic*

"Eric Metaxas clears up many misconceptions, giving priority to Bonhoeffer's own words and actions, in a massive and masterful new biography, *Bonhoeffer: Pastor, Martyr, Prophet, Spy.*"

— *Christianity Today*

"Eric Metaxas tells Bonhoeffer's story with passion and theological sophistication, often challenging revisionist accounts that make Bonhoeffer out to be a 'humanist' or ethicist for whom religious doctrine was easily disposable. . . ."

— *Wall Street Journal*

"Insightful and illuminating, this tome makes a powerful contribution to biography, history and theology."

— *Publisher's Weekly*

"Eric Metaxas is claiming his place as the preeminent biographer of Christianity's most courageous figures."

— Martin Doblmeier, filmmaker, *Bonhoeffer*

"Clearly the definitive work [on Bonhoeffer] . . . One of the greatest biographies I've ever read."

"[D]efinitive and incredibly detailed . . . a powerful, powerful book . . . Highly recommended!"

"One of the finest and most moving biographies I have ever read. Eric Metaxas responds to a great life with a great book."

"Riveting. . . ."

"Metaxas's *Bonhoeffer: Pastor, Martyr, Prophet, Spy* is a modern-day classic that should be on 'best of' lists for the decade. . . ."

"Who is Dietrich Bonhoeffer? He's a guy that you should know. This is a book that you should read."

PRAISE FOR BESTSELLER *AMAZING GRACE*

"Magnificent . . . Metaxas's work will stand as a living landmark."

— The Rev. Floyd Flake, from the
Foreword

"A superb history of the British campaign against slavery . . . *Amazing Grace* will prove to you how great a human effort abolition demanded."

— Stanley Crouch, from the *New York Daily News*

"Metaxas tells Wilberforce's story with a charm and energy reminiscent of a favorite history professor, painting a captivating picture of this era of social reform that revolutionized the world."

— *Bookpage*

"The little-known story of the lifelong struggle of a member of the British Parliament to abolish slavery in the British Empire."

— *USA Today*

"A fine and important book."

— *Chicago Sun-Times*

"A crackling bonfire of truth and clarity . . . Metaxas . . . is an irresistible writer. [He tells this story] with such a sharp eye and ready wit and moral passion that we are caught up in the momentum of it and blown away."

— John Wilson, *Books & Culture*

"[A] spirited, moving account of Wilberforce's life."

— Rich Lowry, *National Review Online*

SEVEN MEN

SEVEN MEN

AND THE SECRET OF
THEIR GREATNESS

ERIC METAXAS

THOMAS NELSON
Since 1798

NASHVILLE   DALLAS   MEXICO CITY   RIO DE JANEIRO

Published in Nashville, Tennessee, by Thomas Nelson. Thomas Nelson is a registered trademark of Thomas Nelson, Inc.

Thomas Nelson, Inc., titles may be purchased in bulk for educational, business, fund-raising, or sales promotional use. For information, please e-mail SpecialMarkets@ThomasNelson.com.

Scripture quotations marked KJV are from the King James Version and are in the public domain.

Scripture quotations marked NIV are from the Holy Bible, New International Version®, NIV®. Copyright © 1973, 1978, 1984 by Biblica, Inc.™ Used by permission of Zondervan. All rights reserved worldwide. www.zondervan.com.

Scripture quotations marked PHILLIPS are from J. B. Phillips: The New Testament in Modern English, Revised Edition. © J. B. Phillips 1958, 1960, 1972. Used by permission of Macmillan Publishing Co., Inc.

Scripture quotations marked NASB are from the New American Standard Bible® © The Lockman Foundation 1960, 1962, 1963, 1968, 1971, 1972, 1973, 1975, 1977, 1995. Used by permission.

Chapter opening photo credits: Wilberforce and Washington, Library of Congress; Liddell and Robinson, Alamy; Bonhoeffer, Art Resource; Colson, Colson Center; Pope John Paul II, Getty Images

Library of Congress Control Number: 2013931701

ISBN: 978-1-59555-469-7
ISBN: 978-1-4002-7605-9 (IE)

Printed in the United States of America

13 14 15 16 17 RRD 6 5 4 3 2 1

THIS BOOK IS DEDICATED
TO MY FATHER, NICHOLAS METAXAS.

Μέ Αγάπη

Contents

Introduction

As most people would concur, the idea of manhood has fallen into some confusion in the last decades. This book hopes to help correct some of that by asking and answering two vitally important questions: First, *what is a man*? And second, *what makes a man great*?

And you'll forgive me if I begin with John Wayne. "The Duke" is obviously not one of the seven men in this book, but many men of my generation have thought of him as something of an icon of manhood and manliness. We still do. But why? What is it about him? Is it the toughness and the swagger? Is it just that he comes across as big and strong and that most men aspire to those qualities? Well, that all has something to do with it, but I actually think his iconic status is because he usually played roles in which his size and strength were used to protect the weak. He was the good guy. He was always strong and tough but never a bully. Somehow watching him on the silver screen said more to generations of men (and women) about what made a man great than endless discussions on the subject. Sometimes a living picture really *is* worth a thousand words. And what we think of John Wayne is a clue to the secret of the greatness of the men in this book.

So this is a book that doesn't talk *about* manhood—at least not after this introduction, which you may skip if you like, although you've already come this far, so why stop?—but that *shows* it in the actual lives of great men. You can talk about right and wrong and good and bad all day long, but ultimately people need to see it. Seeing and studying the actual lives of people is simply the best way to communicate ideas about how to behave and how *not* to behave. We need heroes and role models.

Now, my own personal *greatest* role model is Jesus. And you may have noticed that he didn't just talk. Of course he said a lot of extraordinary things, but he also lived with his disciples for three years. They saw him eat and sleep and perform miracles. They saw him live life and suffer and die. They saw him interact with all kinds of people, including themselves. He lived among them. That's the main way that he communicated himself to the men who would communicate him to the world. That's how he made disciples—who would make disciples, who would make disciples. So from the gospel stories of Jesus' life, you get the idea that seeing a person's life is at least as important as getting a list of lessons from that person. Yes, sermons are important, but seeing the actual life of the guy who gives the sermon might be even more powerful. And you get the idea that how you live affects others. It teaches *them* how to live.

Historically speaking, role models have always been important. Until recently. The ancient Greeks had *Plutarch's Lives*, and in the sixteenth century we got *Foxe's Book of Martyrs*. The message in these and similar books was that these lives were great and worthy of emulation. Having role models and heroes was historically a vital way of helping a new generation know what it should be aiming at. This is one of the main reasons I wrote biographies of William Wilberforce *(Amazing Grace: William Wilberforce and the Heroic Campaign to End Slavery)* and Dietrich Bonhoeffer *(Bonhoeffer: Pastor, Martyr, Prophet, Spy)*. By the way, one of the last books that Bonhoeffer himself was reading just before he died was *Plutarch's Lives*.

So the idea of having heroes and role models has historically been very important; but as I say, somehow this has changed in recent years. *What happened?*

QUESTION AUTHORITY

Part of what happened is that—since roughly the late 1960s—we've adopted the idea that no one is really in a position to say what's right or wrong. So we're loath to point to anyone as a good role model. "Who am I to judge anyone?" has almost become the mantra of our age.

But how did that happen? Well, it's complicated. But it probably has something to do with the Vietnam War and with Watergate. Without a doubt these events helped accelerate a trend toward suspicion of the "official" version of things and of our leaders. Until Vietnam, all previous wars were generally seen as worthy of fighting, and the overwhelming cultural message was that patriotic Americans must do their duty and pitch in and help defend our country and our freedoms. With Vietnam, all that changed. Ditto with Watergate: for the first time in history—thanks mainly to the taped conversations in the White House—we saw and heard a US president not acting "presidential" at all but acting ignobly and venally and shamefully. We heard him use words we wouldn't want our children to use.

So the authority of that president, Richard Nixon, rightfully came under intense scrutiny. But since then, *all* our leaders have been held in deep suspicion. And we've tended to focus on the negative things about famous people. Every negative sound bite of a TV preacher that can be aired will be heard a thousand times more than the good things he's said. It's hard to have heroes in a climate like that.

We've even extended this idea backward through history, so that much of what we hear about our past presidential heroes is negative.

George Washington is no longer thought of mainly as the heroic "Father of Our Country," but as a wealthy landowner who hypocritically owned slaves. Many of us have forgotten the outrageous and spectacular sacrifices that he made and for which every American ought to be endlessly grateful. This is not only disgraceful; it's profoundly harmful to us as a nation. Columbus isn't held up as a brave and intrepid visionary who risked everything to discover a New World. He's considered a murderer of indigenous peoples. It's true that thoughtless idol worship is never a good thing, but being overly critical of men who are otherwise good can also be tremendously harmful. And it has been.

So the very idea of *legitimate* authority has been damaged. Since I was a kid in the seventies, we have had bumper stickers that said "Question Authority." But this didn't just mean we should question whether authority is legitimate, which would be a good idea. No, it seemed to me to go beyond that. It seemed to say that we should question the very idea of authority itself. So you could say that we've gone all the way from foolishly accepting all authority to foolishly rejecting all authority. We've gone from the extreme of being naive to the other extreme of being cynical. The golden mean, where we would question authority *in order to determine whether it was legitimate*, was passed by entirely. We have fled from one icy pole to the other, missing the equator altogether. We are like the person who was so wounded by a betrayal from a member of the opposite sex that he no longer trusts anyone of that sex. Instead of looking for someone who is trustworthy, we've entirely dispensed with the idea of trustworthiness. No one is trustworthy.

This is a very bad place to end up, and in our culture we are paying a harsh price for it. As I've said, people need heroes and role models. Those of us who take the Bible seriously believe that mankind is fallen and that no one is perfect except Jesus. But we also believe that there are some lives that are good examples and some that are bad examples. Can we really believe that certain lives aren't worthy of emulation?

And that others are cautionary tales? Are we really unwilling to say that we shouldn't try to get our children (and ourselves) to see that Abraham Lincoln is worthy of our emulation and Adolf Hitler and Joseph Stalin are not?

Recently I watched an old rerun of *The Rifleman*, starring Chuck Connors. The series ran from 1958 to 1963 and its audience was largely boys. I was absolutely stunned by how the story was clearly trying to communicate what it means to be a real man, a good man, a heroic and brave man. And it was showing the difference between that and being a coward or a bully. This is vital in raising up young men who aspire to do the right thing. But one look at TV today will tell you that this is entirely gone. This book is for everyone, but in writing a book about these seven men, I've thought that young men especially need role models. If we can't point to anyone in history or in our culture whom they should emulate, then they will emulate *whomever.*

Young men who spend their time watching violent movies and playing video games aren't very easily going to become the men they were meant to become. They will drift. They will lose out on the very reason they were brought into this world: to be great, to be heroes themselves. What could be more tragic than that? They won't understand who they are, and they will have no idea how to relate to women, and they will hurt themselves (and probably some women) along the way. So it is vital that we teach them who they are in God's view, and it's vital that we bring back a sense of the heroic. The men in this book are some of my heroes and I am thrilled to be able to share them with others. I hope they will inspire young men to emulate them.

WHAT IS REAL MANHOOD?

At the beginning of this introduction I said that there was a general confusion about manhood. This confusion relates to the larger idea of authority itself coming under attack, which we've just mentioned. Since the father has traditionally been seen as the leader of the family, it only follows that if we've taken the very idea of authority down, we've taken fatherhood down with it.

Can anyone doubt that the idea of fatherhood has declined dramatically in the last forty or so years? One of the most popular TV shows of the 1950s was called *Father Knows Best*. It was a sweet portrayal of a wonderful and in many ways typical American family. The father, played by Robert Young, was the unquestioned authority, but his authority was never harsh or domineering. His strength was a quiet strength. In fact, he was gentle and wise and kind and giving—so much so that just about everyone watching the show wished their dad could be more like that! But of course today we tend to see fathers depicted in the mainstream media either as dunces or as overbearing fools.

There is something vital in the idea of fatherhood and it gives us a clue to the secret of a great man. But we have to point out that a man needn't be an actual father to bear the traits of every good father. Two of the men in this book, Dietrich Bonhoeffer and John Paul II, never married or had children. Even George Washington, who married, never had children of his own. And yet we Americans call him the father of our country. And in the case of Pope John Paul II, the root word from which we get "pope" is *papa*—father. Being a father is not a biological thing. If we think of the fatherhood of God, we get a picture of someone who is strong and loving and who sacrifices himself for those he loves. That's a picture of real fatherhood and real manhood.

SO WHAT IS GOD'S IDEA FOR MANHOOD?

In a world where all authority is questioned and in which our appreciation of real leadership—and especially fatherhood—has been badly damaged, we end up with very little in the way of the heroic in general. As we've said, the idea of manhood itself has become profoundly confused. And as a result of this, instead of God's idea of authentic manhood, we've ended up with two very distorted ideas about manhood.

The first false idea about manhood is the idea of being macho—of being a big shot and using strength to be domineering and to bully those who are weaker. Obviously this is not God's idea of what a real man is. It's someone who has not grown up emotionally, who might be a man on the outside, but who on the inside is simply an insecure and selfish boy.

The second false choice is to be emasculated—to essentially turn away from your masculinity and to pretend that there is no real difference between men and women. Your strength as a man has no purpose, so being strong isn't even a good thing.

God's idea of manhood is something else entirely. It has nothing to do with the two false ideas of either being macho or being emasculated. The Bible says that God made us in his image, male and female, and it celebrates masculinity and femininity. And it celebrates the differences between them. Those differences were God's idea. For one thing, the Bible says that men are generally stronger than women, and of course Saint Peter famously—or infamously—describes women as "the weaker sex." But God's idea of making men strong was so that they would use that strength to protect women and children and anyone else. There's something heroic in that. Male strength is a gift from God, and like all gifts from God, it's always and everywhere meant to be used to bless others. In Genesis 12:1–3, God tells Abraham that he will bless him *so that Abraham can bless others.* All blessings and every gift—and strength is a gift—are God's gifts, to be used for his purposes, which means to bless others. So men are meant to use their strength to protect and bless those who are weaker. That can mean other men who need help or it can mean women and children. True strength is always strength given over to God's purposes.

But because men have sometimes used their strength selfishly, there has been a backlash against the whole idea of masculine strength. It has been seen—and portrayed—as something negative. If you buy into that idea, then you realize the only way to deal with it is to work against it, to try to weaken men, because whatever strength they have will be used to harm others. This leads to the emasculated idea of men. Strength is denigrated because it can be used for ill. So we live in a culture where strength is feared and where there is a sense that—to protect the weak—strength itself must be weakened. When this happens, the heroic and true nature of strength is much forgotten. It leads to a world of men who aren't really men. Instead they are just two kinds of boys: boasting, loud-mouthed bullies or soft, emasculated pseudo-men. Women feel that they must be "empowered" and must never rely on men for strength. It's a lot like a socialistic idea, where "power" and "strength" are redistributed—taken away from men and given to women, to even things out. Of course it doesn't work that way. Everyone loses.

The knight in shining armor who does all he can to protect others, the gentleman who lays down his cloak or opens a door for a lady—these are Christian ideals of manliness. Jesus said that he who would lead must be the servant of all. It's the biblical idea of servant leadership. The true leader gives himself to the people he leads. The good shepherd lays down his life for his sheep. Jesus washed the feet of the disciples. Jesus died for those he loves. That is God's idea of strength and leadership and blessing. It's something to be used in the service of others. So God's idea of masculine strength gives us the idea of a chivalrous gentleman toward women, not a bully or someone who sees no difference between himself and them.

CHIVALRY AND HEROISM ARE NOT DEAD

Last summer, there was a terrible shooting at a movie theater. Twelve people who had gone to a midnight showing of the most recent Batman movie were senselessly murdered by what can only be described as a madman. But of all the things that have been said about this tragic event, what struck me more than anything was that three young men died protecting their girlfriends from the madman's bullets. Something caused them to risk losing their lives for a young woman. Why did they do that? What does that say about manhood?

In the killer, you have a perfect picture of evil, which is the opposite of love. It is a picture of someone using power (in this case his firearm) to destroy, to harm. But in the three young men, you have a picture of strength expressed as love, which is the opposite of evil. You see men using their power and their strength to protect. In the case of the first you see someone doing something that is unfathomably selfish, someone who seems to see no value in others, and whose actions reflect that judgment. In the second you see three men doing something that is unfathomably selfless. Why did they use their strength and power to help someone else? What was that instinct, and why did they follow it?

The stories in this book are the stories of men who followed that latter path, who seemed to know that at the heart of what it is to be a man is that idea of being selfless, of putting your greatest strength at God's disposal, and of sometimes surrendering something that is yours for a larger purpose—of giving what is yours in the service of others.

HAVING COURAGE MEANS HAVING HEART

I was an English major in college, and now I'm a writer—so I hope you won't mind a brief etymological digression. It doesn't matter if you don't know exactly what that is, but the point I want to make is very important.

We say that the selfless acts of those men in the movie theater—and the selfless acts of most people everywhere—are courageous. Strength in the service of others is courageous. But did you know that the word *courage* comes from the Latin *cor*, which means "heart"? So to have courage simply means to have "heart." Of course the Bible often exhorts people to "take heart" or to "be of good courage." The meaning is effectively the same. So to have heart *means* to have courage. This is God's idea of strength, to have a heart like a lion. A man who has heart can be described as *lionhearted*.

You may notice that the false macho idea of manliness sees having "heart" as a weak, soft thing. It misses the true idea of what it is to have heart. Instead, the false macho concept of manhood substitutes having something else. Hint: it starts with a "b." Second hint: the Spanish word is *cojones*. But notice that this concept of manhood reduces God's idea of a noble and heroic man to a sexual level. It puts us in mind of apes and goats, but not of lions. Did you ever read the C. S. Lewis essay titled "Men Without Chests"? Lewis understood that large-hearted men, men "with chests," were real men. It's about having a chest and a heart. Until we realize that God is concerned with the size of our hearts and not that of our genital apparati, we can never understand God's idea of true masculinity.

So what is "heart"? It's courage, but courage to do what? The courage to do the right thing when all else tells you not to do it. The courage to rise above your surroundings and circumstances. The courage to be God's idea of a real man and to give of yourself for others when it costs you to do so and when everything tells you to look out for yourself first.

WHY DID I CHOOSE THESE SEVEN MEN?

Anyone reading this book must wonder why I chose these seven men. Of course this is not a definitive list. There is great subjectivity in these choices. There are many, many more whom I would have liked to include and whom I hope to include in future volumes. But in this first volume I was looking for seven men who had all evinced one particular quality: that of surrendering themselves to a higher purpose, of giving something away that they might have kept. All of them did this in one way or another. Doing this is noble and admirable, and it takes courage and it usually takes faith. Each of the seven men in this book have that quality.

Let me explain briefly what I mean for each of them.

As you'll soon see when you read about him, *George Washington*

(1732–1799) once voluntarily gave up extraordinary power. He actually could have become a king, when being a king really meant something; but he selflessly refused the honor. Such a sacrifice is almost unfathomable to us today. But Washington knew there was something even greater than power. To do the noble thing, the heroic thing, the right thing—for him, that was greater than becoming powerful. He surrendered all that power for the sake of something nobler: he did it for the sake of his new country and for millions yet to be born. If he hadn't done it, that country might not have lasted very long. So anyone who is an American is a direct beneficiary of what this great man did. This is not hyperbole. What he did affected you, personally. He gave up a sure thing to do the right thing, and today he is deservedly regarded to be one of the greatest heroes in the history of the world.

Similarly, *William Wilberforce* (1759–1833) gave up the chance to be prime minister of England. Many have said that he "put principle above party" and gave up becoming prime minister. But for what did he surrender the prize of that office? He gave it up for a cause that to him was far greater than becoming the leader of the greatest empire in the world at that time. He gave up his life for the sake of African slaves, people who could give him nothing in return. But Wilberforce knew that what God had given up for him was far greater, so he did what he did for the Africans he would never meet, and for God.

This man's conversion to the Christian faith changed everything for him. Suddenly he saw everything differently. Suddenly he realized that everything he had been given—wealth and power and influence and connections and intelligence and a gift of oratory—was a gift from God. And he realized that it was a gift to be used for others. The choice was his, of course, but when you really know that God has given you something for others, it's hard not to use it for others. Wilberforce knew that taking everything he had been given and using it to improve the lives of others was the very reason he had been born. And by devoting himself to this for five decades of his life, he became one of the most important human beings who ever lived.

He changed the world in a way that would have been unthinkable at the time.

The 1982 movie *Chariots of Fire* tells the story of *Eric Liddell* (1902–1945) who gave up the acclaim of millions to honor God. It is one of the most extraordinary stories in the history of sports. But it doesn't involve any athletic action. In fact, it involves deliberate athletic *non*-action. It was the historic decision by a devoutly Christian young man to forgo the one thing that everyone said he should want— and deserved—namely, the opportunity to win an Olympic gold medal in the one event in which he was most likely to win it. But God came first, and Liddell surrendered his best chance for Olympic gold. And, as you'll discover, that's only half of his story.

Then there is the brilliant and heroic German pastor and theologian *Dietrich Bonhoeffer* (1906–1945), who courageously defied the Nazis and surrendered his freedom and safety time and time again. He did that most notably in 1939 when he made the fateful decision to leave the safety of America to return to Germany, simply because he felt that was what God wanted him to do. Ultimately, he gave up his life. His willingness to do that has inspired countless people to do the right thing in thousands of situations, and Bonhoeffer's story is inspiring them still.

Jackie Robinson (1919–1972) was given the opportunity to do something historic when he was chosen to be the man who broke the so-called color barrier in professional baseball. But in order to do this, he had to surrender something very few men would have the strength to surrender: he would have to give up the right to fight back against some of the most vicious insults against his race that anyone has ever heard. It must have taken superhuman effort, but with faith in God, and with a desire to bless unknown millions who would have the opportunity to follow in his footsteps, he did just that. He made a great sacrifice for people he would never meet. He thought of his wife and his children, whom he knew, but he also thought of all the others who would benefit from his doing the right thing, and he suffered greatly to do what he did. Because of his courage and heroism, he is in this book of great men.

Karol Wojtyla—whom we know as *Pope John Paul II* (1920–2005)—surrendered his whole life to God in what many would think of as the most typical way: he became a priest and decided to serve God. He became a bishop, an archbishop, a cardinal, and finally, in 1978, the pope. But he was not an ambitious man. He wasn't in it for the power. He gave up his right to himself. He even gave up his right to dignity. When he grew old, he went before the whole world as a picture of a man weakened by Parkinson's disease, but who nonetheless courageously continued to appear before the world, even in that weakened state. As a result, he showed in his own life what he professed with his words, that a human being is sacred in God's eyes. Even in our weakened state, and *especially* in our weakened state, we are children of God. He was a picture of courage and of heroic consistency, a man who practiced what he preached.

The one man in this book I had the privilege to know personally was *Chuck Colson* (1931–2012). In the beginning of his life, Chuck was a man who was not exactly headed for inclusion in a book like this one. He was tremendously ambitious, but he seemed to seek power for its own sake, or for *his* own sake. Eventually he amassed a tremendous amount of it, as special counsel to the president of the United States, Richard Nixon. This was a heady thing for a man not yet forty, and what he did with that power was his great undoing. But when, in the scandal of Watergate, that power was finally stripped from him, Chuck Colson found the real reason for his life and for life in general. And when his role in Watergate threatened to send him to prison, he didn't blink. His faith was so strong that he knew the only thing to do was to trust God so completely that it would look crazy to the rest of the world. And it did look crazy. But he didn't care about what anyone thought—except God. He was playing to the proverbial audience of One and he refused a plea bargain that would have made his life much easier during that time. Then he voluntarily pled guilty when he didn't have to—and went to prison as a result. But he knew that when you give everything to God, only then are you truly free. His is a true picture of greatness for all of us.

THE GREATEST

In my humble estimation, the men in this book are some of the greatest men who have ever lived. So if you get to know their stories, your life will be immeasurably richer. It is my fondest hope that these short biographies would lead you to read longer biographies of these great men. I hope you would want to study these lives—and not just study them but emulate them. It is my prayer that those who read this book would be inspired to become real heroes, to become great men in their own generation.

You may read the seven stories of these seven men in the chronological order in which they appear here, or you might skip around. It doesn't matter. These chapters can stand alone as well as they can stand together.

— Eric Metaxas
New York City
October 2012

ONE
George Washington

1732–99

et me begin the first biography in this book by saying that even if the seven great men discussed within its pages were not in chronological order, I probably still would have started with George Washington. When it comes to true greatness, Washington's tough to beat. But someone's greatness can sometimes lend him an aura of such outsized fame that we begin to think of him not as a real person but as a cartoon superhero or as a legend. That's often the case with Washington.

As you know, he has a state named after him. (Do I need to say which?) And he has our nation's capital city named after him; he has a soaring obelisk monument in that city; his birthday is a national holiday; and he has a huge bridge named after him right here in my hometown of New York City. And if all these things aren't impressive enough, his face is on the dollar bill! (Perhaps you already knew that.) So who really thinks of him as an actual flesh-and-blood human being who struggled as we all struggle and who put on his breeches one leg at a time? That's the problem with being *that* famous. People often don't really think about you as a person at all.

If you do think of him, you probably think of George Washington as that old guy with the somewhat sour expression on the afore-mentioned dollar bill. In that overfamiliar picture, sporting heavily powdered hair and a lace-trimmed shirt, he looks almost as much like an old woman as an old man.

But what I've discovered is that this famous portrait has given many of us an outrageously false picture of who Washington actually was. It presents him as an elderly man with chronic denture discom-fort, who looks none too happy for it. But the reality is completely different.

What if I told you that in his day, George Washington was consid-ered about the manliest man most people had ever seen? No kidding. Virtually everyone who knew him or saw him seemed to say so. He was tall and powerful. He was also both fearless and graceful. On the field of battle, he had several horses shot out from under him; on the dance floor, he was a much sought-after partner.

There's so much to say about Washington that it's hard to know where to begin. For one thing, he was a man of tremendous contra-dictions. For example, the man who became known as the father of our country never fathered children himself. And he lost his own father when he was a young boy. The man who was viewed as deeply honorable actually told some real whoppers when he was a young man, despite Parson Weems's fictitious episode by the cherry tree: "I cannot tell a lie." More than anyone else, he is responsible for freeing American colonists from the greatest military power on earth—the British Empire—and yet he held some three hundred black men, women, and children in bondage at Mount Vernon.[1]

But here's the biggest contradiction: Washington was an extremely ambitious young man who worked hard to achieve fame, glory, land, and riches—yet at a pivotal moment in American history, he did something so selfless that it's difficult to fully fathom. It's principally because of this one thing that he's included in this book.

So what did he do? In a nutshell, he voluntarily gave up incredible power. When you know the details of his sacrifice, it's hard to believe that he did what he did of his own free will. And yet he did it. The temptation *not* to surrender all that power must have been extraordinary. There were many good reasons not to surrender it, but history records that he somehow did. Somehow he made an impossibly grand sacrifice—and in doing so he dramatically changed the history of the world. Had Washington not been willing to do it, America as we know it almost certainly would not exist. That's not hyperbole.

This is why contemporary memorials to Washington describe him as an American Moses, as someone loaned to Americans from God. He was the right man for his time—arguably the only man who could have successfully birthed the American Experiment. If you wonder whether one person's actions can matter, and if you wonder whether character matters, you needn't look any further than the story of George Washington. So here it is.

◆ ◆ ◆

George Washington was born on February 22, 1732, in what is now Westmoreland County, Virginia, the first son of Mary Ball Washington and tobacco farmer Augustine Washington. George had two older half-brothers, Augustine and Lawrence, and one half sister, Jane, who were children from his father's first marriage. George also had five full younger siblings: Samuel, Elizabeth, John, Charles, and Mildred.

Augustine and Lawrence were sent to England for their educations, but George's father died when George was just eleven, making an English education for him financially impossible. He would regret this deficit in his education throughout his long life. George's brother Lawrence, who was fourteen years older, became a father figure to him, someone whose advice the young George would listen to. In 1751, Lawrence took nineteen-year-old George to Barbados, where Lawrence hoped to be cured of tuberculosis. Alas, George contracted smallpox on this trip. Although the disease was dangerous, it actually turned out to be a hugely fortunate occurrence; George was then inoculated from the disease at an early age, thereby preventing him from future attacks of it when he was a general. During the Revolutionary War, large numbers of soldiers died of disease rather than enemy attacks.

As a boy growing into manhood, George frequently visited Lawrence's home on the Potomac River, which was named Mount Vernon. He also frequently visited Belvoir, owned by Lawrence's in-laws. As one biographer put it, at Mount Vernon and Belvoir, "George discovered a world that he had never known."[2] In particular, Belvoir "was a grand structure, an architectural showcase gracefully adorned with exquisite molding and rich paneling and decorated tastefully with furniture and accessories from England."[3] George "was stirred by the people" in these homes, "people of influence," adults "who were well-read and thoughtful, men who were accustomed to wielding power."[4]

Young George determined to turn himself into one of them—especially someone like Lawrence, who was not only a distinguished war hero but also adjutant general of Virginia, a member of the Virginia legislature, the House of Burgesses, and by marriage, a member of the socially prominent Fairfax family. George threw himself into learning proper etiquette, reading serious books, dressing properly, and improving his character. He also eventually shot up to be roughly six-foot-three, this making him much taller than most of his contemporaries and giving him the heroic, statuesque appearance of a born commander.

Given his future career, it's certainly ironic that George's mother fought his efforts, at age fourteen, to become a commissioned officer in the Royal Navy. She thought such a life would be too harsh for her son, so George decided to learn to become a surveyor. He was fiercely intent on acquiring property and wealth, and a surveying career could lead to quick riches in land and money. By the time he turned twenty, George owned some twenty-five hundred acres of Virginia's frontier land.[5]

But that same year—1752—tragedy struck. George's beloved brother Lawrence lost his battle with tuberculosis. Lawrence's wife and daughter also died within a few years. This meant that George would ultimately inherit Mount Vernon—an estate he would ambitiously enlarge and improve during the next four decades.

When he was twenty-one, George once again turned his attention toward the possibility of a military career. Through the intervention of influential friends, and despite the fact that George had no military experience, Virginia's governor appointed him commander of the southernmost military district of Virginia, a post that gave him the rank of major. This was an unexpected development, and it would not be long before George had an opportunity to test his mettle in a dramatic—and ultimately historic—way.

On the horizon loomed the French and Indian War, in which the French and several tribes of native Americans joined forces against Great Britain (including the Anglo-Americans) for what was then called the Ohio Territory—a vast area, much larger than the current US state of Ohio. Both France and Britain claimed this territory, and in 1750, France sent an army there and built Fort Le Boeuf, about fifteen miles from Lake Erie, in what is today the northwestern corner of Pennsylvania. This aggressive move by the French infuriated many Virginians, particularly those who owned territory in the region. What to do? The governor of Virginia, Robert Dinwiddie, consulted Crown officials in London, who advised him to send an emissary to the French, letting them know in no uncertain terms that the territory belonged to the English and that they had better remove their troops posthaste.

When young George Washington learned of the need for a messenger to travel through the mountains and wilderness during that upcoming winter, he immediately put himself forward as the man for the job. Governor Dinwiddie accepted Washington's offer and also gave George a number of other responsibilities. He was to spy out the land and the size of the French force. He was also instructed to consult with the so-called "half-king," the chief of the Seneca tribe, about the possibility of their joining with the British against the French, in the event that war should break out. And he was to attempt to find a good location for building an English fort in the area—something that was an absolute necessity if the Ohio Company, a Virginia land specula- tion company, were to "gain legal title to the hundreds of thousands of acres it coveted in the Ohio Country."[6]

So twenty-one-year-old George left with the governor's letter and six companions. They spent weeks hiking the many miles from Virginia to Ohio, through the endless terrain of winter snow, headed for Fort Le Boeuf.

When they got close to their destination, a French patrol met them and escorted Washington and his men to the fort. The French treated them civilly, as was the custom. They welcomed them, fed them, received and read the letter George delivered, and then gave George their response to take back to Virginia. But as George suspected from conversations that he overheard, the response was not what the English hoped. The French resolutely declared that the land was theirs. If that was true, the two world powers would soon be at war.

George and his men returned home with the letter—in which the French indeed claimed the land as their own—and he prepared an account of his adventure, which was published in colonial news- papers. His fame also spread through London when his memoir was published in pamphlet form under the title *The Journal of Major George Washington*. It was the first time the British would hear of this valiant young man, and obviously not the last.

Faced with French defiance, the House of Burgesses was forced to take action. The members voted to fund what they named the Virginia Regiment, a three-hundred-man volunteer army. This regiment was to travel to the Ohio Valley to assist in building a fort, which Dinwiddie considered essential to protect British interests. The Virginia Regiment was to be led by an experienced British soldier named Colonel Joshua Fry. The ambitious Washington pressed political friends to promote him to the rank of lieutenant colonel, which they succeeded in doing, and so he joined the regiment with this rank.

But Fry could not immediately leave Virginia, so it was the young Washington himself who was charged with leading 186 men into western Pennsylvania. Upon learning that the French had sent one thousand soldiers to build what they would name Fort Duquesne, Washington was in a quandary. He had far fewer men at his disposal than did the French. He had been urging Indians to join the British, but he had no way of knowing whether they actually would.

He also feared negative repercussions if, in effect, he surrendered before meeting up with French troops. Should he wait for Colonel Fry and reinforcements? Adding to Washington's uneasiness were the stealthy nighttime sounds of men nearby. Were they deserters or French soldiers?

Indian scouts gave Washington a further confusing message. They said that a force of French soldiers was headed in Washington's direction, hoping to meet Washington and attack the English. Washington decided to stay where he was, and two days later he received more news from Christopher Gist, who had traveled with Washington on his previous trip into the Ohio wilderness, that a French party of about fifty men was approaching. These soldiers "had invaded [Gist's] nearby wilderness cabin, vowing to kill his cow and smash 'everything in the house.'"[7]

As one historian notes, the inexperienced Washington made "a crucial decision, and one that violated Dinwiddie's instructions to keep the army within its fortifications."[8] Washington sent half his men ahead and then learned from an Indian ally that the French had been spotted not far away. Washington took forty of his men on a rainy night march, determined to make a surprise attack. What took place the next morning in May 1754 simply boggles the imagination.

On their arrival, Washington discovered thirty-two French soldiers calmly preparing their breakfast. For some unknown reason, Washington ordered his men to open fire, and a dozen of the French were immediately slaughtered. Once the smoke cleared, French ensign Joseph Coulon de Villiers, Sieur de Jumonville, attempted to explain to Washington that his troops were on a diplomatic mission. But at the very moment that "Jumonville read this ultimatum, things got immeasurably worse: the Half-King stepped forward, split open [Jumonville's] head with a hatchet, then dipped his hands into the skull, rinsed them with the victim's brains, and scalped him."[9]

Washington would never forget this unspeakably grotesque scene or the demonic horrors of the chaos that ensued. The Seneca traveling with him now viciously attacked and scalped the wounded French, impaling the head of one man on a stake. "Immobilized either by bloodlust or the awful sights that he was beholding for the first time, Washington made no attempt to stop the carnage," writes biographer John Ferling.[10] It's possible Washington did not want to antagonize the Indians by attempting to stop their atrocities.

After it was all over, Washington wrote to Dinwiddie, claiming the French soldiers were actually "Spyes of the worst sort"[11] who intended to prepare the way for an attack by the French. This may well have been true—the diplomatic message may indeed have been cover—but knowing that his French prisoners would have their own story to tell about what happened, Washington warned Dinwiddie not to believe them.

To be sure, Washington had more to worry about than possible condemnation by Dinwiddie. When French leaders at Fort Duquesne learned of the carnage that had taken place against their men, they would certainly seek revenge. Washington immediately ordered his men to begin construction of what he would call Fort Necessity. But the fort's location was rather ill chosen: forests and hills closely surrounded the fort, which meant that the French would be able to get close to it and shoot the English like fish in the proverbial barrel.

This was precisely what happened. Some nine hundred French and Indian fighters arrived under the command of Louis Coulon de Villiers, who was the brother of Jumonville, and immediately opened fire. After they had killed or wounded a full quarter of Washington's men, Villiers asked Washington if he would like to surrender. Washington agreed to do so and—worse from the standpoint of his record—he signed a document in which he confessed that Jumonville had been murdered.

Washington again sent misleading reports of the battle, falsely claiming that more than three hundred French had become casualties (in reality, they suffered only nineteen) and that the English defeat was due to inexperienced men and dwindling supplies. Washington "never, then or later, admitted to any errors on his part," writes Ferling.[12] Washington also claimed that the man who acted as translator between the French and the English was incompetent and possibly corrupt; otherwise he never would have "confessed" to the murder of Jumonville. Again, it's difficult to know what really happened.

The French and Indian War, as it would henceforth be known, and which these battles launched, would last five years. Despite patently bad decision making, the young Washington's "virtues stood out amid the temporary wreckage of his reputation. With unflagging resolution, he had kept his composure in battle, even when surrounded by piles of corpses. . . . Utterly fearless, he faced down dangers and seemed undeterred by obstacles."[13] In the weeks after the debacle, "condemnation of Washington gradually gave way to widespread acknowledgment that he had confronted terrifying odds at Fort Necessity."[14]

◆ ◆ ◆

The now twenty-two-year-old Washington, doubtless licking his wounds, retired to Mount Vernon. But it would not be very long before he had a chance to redeem himself.

In 1755, the British sent General Edward Braddock, two infantry regiments, and seven hundred provincial soldiers to take Fort Duquesne from the French. Washington, who was experienced in traveling in the wilderness and in communicating with Indians, was invited to join this expedition and to serve on General Braddock's staff.

On July 9, after fording the Monongahela River, Braddock and an advance force of fourteen hundred men encountered a huge force of French and Indians. The French soldiers, who had learned how to fight Indian-style, raced into the woods, surrounded the British, and rained deadly fire on them, killing or wounding 976 men, including Braddock. It was a tremendous slaughter, "the worst defeat suffered by the British in America prior to the War of Independence."[15] But in this hellish hail of bullets and death, Washington first showed himself as a man of legendary courage and passion on the field of battle. History records that "Washington alone of Braddock's aides emerged unscathed, though his hat and coat were riddled with bullet holes and two horses were shot from beneath him. Washington never ran. He stood and fought with great valor."[16]

It seems genuinely miraculous that Washington survived that day, and the courage involved in staying amidst such gunfire as would put holes in his hat and coat—and not one but two horses—is nothing less than superlatively heroic. As a result of Washington's spectacular gallantry during this battle, Governor Dinwiddie asked him to command Virginia's now much larger army. He would have the rank of colonel. Washington and his men of the Virginia army spent the next several years fighting the Indians, who continued to attack settlements and murder the families living there. Washington often complained about the lack of adequate men, equipment, and Indian allies, along with the fact that they were fighting a defensive rather than an offensive war. And as military leaders often do today, he complained that the civilian leaders who knew little about battlefield tactics were making the wrong decisions.

In 1757, the British government decided that to finally drive the French from Fort Duquesne, it would send three armies to America, one of them under the leadership of Brigadier General John Forbes. Washington now presided over two Virginia regiments of some two thousand men, and Forbes assigned him to lead one of these three brigades. Learning from captured enemy soldiers that Fort Duquesne was lightly garrisoned, Forbes, intent on capturing it, sent twenty-five hundred men under Washington's command to do it. But when they at long last arrived in late 1758, they discovered that the French had fled the fort after burning it. The Americans later learned that the French had become uneasy after their Indian allies left them and decided that their best option was to destroy the fort and leave. There was obviously little glory in Washington's victory, but it was a victory nonetheless. And thus would end the military career of the twenty-six-year-old George Washington—or so he then thought.

Shortly afterward, Washington resigned his commission, to the sorrow of his officers, who had become extremely fond of him. Many of them participated in a moving farewell tribute, noting his commitment to justice, as well as his loyalty, fairness, sincerity, and other positive qualities. Few could question that Washington's disciplined and courageous leadership had inspired them to give their best efforts.

Washington was deeply touched by this farewell. He thanked the men, saying that he did so with "true affection for the honor you have done me, for if I have acquired any reputation, it is from you I derive it."[17] This was typical of the graciousness that would mark him in future years.

But now that he was leaving the military, just what would become of this promising young man?

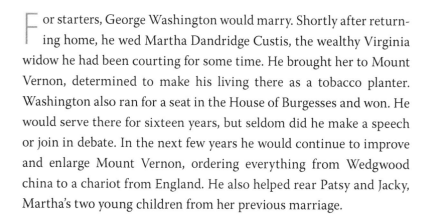

For starters, George Washington would marry. Shortly after returning home, he wed Martha Dandridge Custis, the wealthy Virginia widow he had been courting for some time. He brought her to Mount Vernon, determined to make his living there as a tobacco planter. Washington also ran for a seat in the House of Burgesses and won. He would serve there for sixteen years, but seldom did he make a speech or join in debate. In the next few years he would continue to improve and enlarge Mount Vernon, ordering everything from Wedgwood china to a chariot from England. He also helped rear Patsy and Jacky, Martha's two young children from her previous marriage.

But things were happening in the world beyond Mount Vernon that wouldn't let George Washington remain as he was for long. In 1764, Britain's passage of the Revenue Act, which taxed rum, wine, coffee, tea, molasses, sugar, and tobacco, enraged most Americans, even though the taxes were intended to pay for Britain's defense of America from future attacks by the French or Indians. After all, no American had a seat in Parliament, and taxation without representation was not something they were eager to accept.

When, in 1765, Parliament passed the Stamp Act (a tax on official documents and pamphlets among other things), the outrage against Great Britain increased. For one thing, there were riots. Parliament repealed the Stamp Act in 1766, but it then promptly reinfuriated the Americans by passing the Townshend Acts in 1767, which taxed paper, tea, glass, lead, and paint. American boycotts of many British imports ensued, costing the British much lost income.

In 1770, the Boston Massacre took place, in which British soldiers killed five colonists, further inflaming American feeling against the presence of British troops on their soil. And in 1773, the British imposed the Tea Act, which led to the Boston Tea Party—an act of protest that amuses most Americans today, but that in some of its lesser-known and gruesome details horrified many, including George Washington. Nonetheless, Washington knew that things had come to a point at which something had to be done. Until now he had mostly listened quietly while other members of the Virginia House of Burgesses expressed their wrath at the escalating British abuses. Even he "was prepared for a strident response against Britain's imperial policies, if a majority of colonists were of like mind."[18]

Indeed, they were. The American colonists passionately believed that Parliament had absolutely no legal authority to impose taxes on them. So in August of 1774, Washington was among seven men chosen to represent Virginia in Philadelphia at the newly formed Continental Congress. The Congress decided on a boycott of all British-made goods, to be supported by the thirteen colonies. And the congressmen made plans for activating each colony's militia if the need should arise, which it soon and certainly did.

It was on that now famous date, "the eighteenth of April in '75," that a Boston silversmith named Paul Revere rode through the night to warn his fellow colonists of the imminent arrival of British troops. The British had sent a thousand soldiers to confiscate arms and arrest Revolutionary leaders. The next morning, the curtain rose on that great War of Independence we now call the American Revolution. Most of us know the story of how American fathers and husbands left the warmth of their beds to fiercely resist British troops at Lexington and Concord. The casualties from these historic clashes were shocking at the time, especially given the fact that war had not yet been declared. Nearly three hundred British soldiers and one hundred Massachusetts militiamen were killed or wounded.[19]

Learning of the conflict, Washington memorably mused in a letter to his friend George Fairfax,

> Unhappy it is though to reflect, that a Brother's Sword has been sheathed in a Brother's breast, and that, the once happy and peaceful plains of America are either to be drenched with Blood, or Inhabited by Slaves. Sad alternative! But can a virtuous Man hesitate in his choice?[20]

News of the battles electrified the thirteen colonies; thousands of New England militiamen poured into Boston, besieging the British in an effort not only to trap them within the city but also to force them, through a shortage of food and other supplies, to board their ships and leave, preferably forever.

In what became known as the Battle of Bunker Hill—which the English technically won—the angry Americans, who happened to be very good shots and who broke the rules of military etiquette by targeting officers, forced the British to pay a heavy price: about one thousand

British soldiers were killed or wounded, while the Americans suffered around five hundred casualties.[21]

That May, the Second Continental Congress met. Its members realized that the colonies could not fight independently of one another; the thirteen militias needed to be transformed into a single, national army. But who would lead it? On June 19, 1775, George Washington answered the call. He was forty-three years old.

But we must wonder, what exactly was it about Washington that put him forward as the first choice of the Continental Congress? John Adams joked that he met every qualification: he was tall and handsome, and he moved gracefully—qualities evidently lacking in the other candidates. But there were serious reasons too. For one thing, Washington was rich, so he was considered immune to enemy bribes. That was an important consideration at the time. And he had a sparkling reputation; he seemed to make a grand impression wherever he went. As one Connecticut observer noted, "He seems discreet and virtuous, no harum-scarum, ranting, swearing fellow, but sober, steady, and calm."[22]

Addressing Congress at Philadelphia's State House, Washington—who knew it would take a miracle to beat the British—said with his typical humility: "I do not think myself equal to the command I [am] honored with, [but] as the Congress desire it I will enter upon the momentous duty, & give every power I possess in their service & for the Support of the glorious Cause."[23]

Washington revealed his apprehensions about the militiamen's lack of experience, who were not trained soldiers but farmers and tradespeople. Writing to his brother-in-law shortly after he was given his command, Washington said, "I can answer but for three things: a firm belief in the justice of our cause; close attention in the prosecution of it; and the strictest integrity. If these cannot supply the places of ability and experience, the cause will suffer."[24]

After making final preparations for his new duties and bidding Martha good-bye, Washington fatefully mounted his horse and rode from Philadelphia to Cambridge, Massachusetts.

◆ ◆ ◆

What followed, from the summer of 1775 through 1781, were six long years of sporadic fighting from Saratoga to Boston, from Trenton to Long Island; from Moore's Creek Bridge, North Carolina, to Bennington, Vermont; Savannah, Chesapeake Bay, and, finally, Yorktown.

The details of the Revolutionary War have become iconic; the bleak winter of 1777–1778 at Valley Forge, where many of Washington's troops died from sickness. The crossing of the Delaware River that was part of the daring Christmas night attack, surprising hungover Hessian mercenaries and winning a victory when America desperately needed one.

Washington stoically dealt with endless difficulties: constant troop shortages; the disturbing betrayal of a trusted colleague, General Benedict Arnold; attempts at assassination; and efforts to capture him. But somehow—many would say quite miraculously—Washington shaped up a ragtag collection of underfed, underpaid, and underarmed men into the enviable fighting force that (with a little help from the French) vanquished the most powerful military force that had ever existed.

One biographer notes that in the final big battle of the war, in Yorktown, Virginia, "Washington dismounted, stood in the line of fire, and watched."[25] No one disputes that he was tremendously brave. Many times throughout his military career, he fearlessly put himself in harm's way, despite the fact that when the tall general mounted his horse, he provided enemy soldiers with an especially visible and tempting target.

◆ ◆ ◆

Many of us have seen the famous painting of General Washington piously praying on one knee beside his horse. Biographers tell us that there is no record of Washington ever having done anything like this. But there is no doubt that Washington was a deeply religious man and that he relied on his faith to help him when making decisions about the war. So what's depicted in that painting certainly could have taken place.

Washington's nephew, George Lewis, was an inadvertent witness to his uncle's faith. He related what he saw to Washington biographer Jared Sparks, who wrote:

> Mr. Lewis said he had accidentally witnessed [the general's] private devotions in his library both morning and evening; that on these occasions he had seen him in a kneeling position with a Bible open before him and that he believed such to have been his daily practice.[26]

As Ron Chernow relates in *Washington: A Life*, when, during the Revolutionary War, General Robert Porterfield "delivered an urgent message to Washington" he "found him on his knees, engaged in his morning's devotions."[27]

A lifelong churchgoer, Washington served for twenty-two years as a vestryman of Truro Parish and also served as a churchwarden whose duties included assisting the poor. Friends, such as John Marshall, knew Washington to be "a sincere believer in the Christian faith, and a truly devout man."[28] Washington also believed that God had a special purpose for his life, and he spoke of his belief that Providence had saved him from being killed in various early battles precisely because God had a purpose for him.

Washington's charity toward others is also well documented. Before leaving to command the American forces in the Revolutionary War, he made a point of telling his estate manager to continue looking after beggars who showed up at Mount Vernon: "Let the hospitality of the house with respect to the poor be kept up. Let no one go hungry away . . . provided it does not encourage them in idleness."[29]

Chernow notes,

> We know that the Washingtons tried to practice anonymous charity even when it would have been politically expedient to advertise

it loudly. Washington's secretary, Tobias Lear, recorded hundreds of individuals, churches, and other charities that, unbeknownst to the public, benefited from presidential largesse. Even leftovers from the executive mansion were transferred to a prison for needy inmates.[30]

Many of us are familiar with the oft-quoted lines in Washington's Farewell Address in 1796: "Of all the dispositions and habits which lead to political prosperity, religion and morality are indispensable supports." But we're likely less familiar with the rest of the passage, in which Washington warns that "reason and experience both forbid us to expect that national morality can prevail in exclusion of religious principle."[31] As "national morality" is at the heart of self-government, this is an especially important statement.

It says much about Washington's character that, following General Cornwallis's surrender, Washington told his men to treat their defeated foes with respect and to refrain from shouting taunts and insults at them. "It is sufficient for us that we witness their humiliation," he said. "Posterity will huzza for us."[32]

There was something about Washington's heroic, humble, fearless, and fair example that inspired fierce devotion in the men under his leadership. In fact, the respect, admiration, and love his men had for him increased during the years of war. Biographer David Adler writes, "His men followed him barefoot through the snow at Trenton. They wintered with him at Valley Forge without proper clothes, food, or firewood. Surely, they fought not only for independence, but also for Washington."[33]

◆ ◆ ◆

But it was what George Washington did after the war that for all time marks him as someone who stands in the very first rank of the great men of history.

One might well ask: When the heroic struggle for independence was finally won, what next? How should the great man who carried this new nation to its nascent victory be rewarded? How should his epochal triumph be crowned? Some talked of doing so literally, of crowning Washington as King George I of America—or at the very least, of making him into a kinglike figure. Even those who disliked this idea feared that with all Washington had done, it was somehow inevitable: he had simply earned it. And those who bitterly opposed the idea expected Washington to take what he thought belonged to him. They pointed to Washington's desire to maintain a standing army as evidence that he planned a military coup after the war. As they saw it, newly independent America would end up with a military dictatorship, with Washington as dictator in chief.

Yet Washington was that rarest of men on the expansive stage of history because he would have none of it. His attitude toward the idea that he should grab the reins of civilian power is dramatically illustrated in an incident that reveals, as few others do, the singular greatness of George Washington.

It took place in March 1783. The war was over and won, but the mood among the officers of the Continental Army in Newburgh, New York—Washington's headquarters at that time—had turned decidedly ugly. This was mainly because Congress was quite broke and would not likely be able to honor its promise to compensate the soldiers for their years of arduous service to their country. It seemed Congress wasn't even able to provide pensions. This was a tremendously harsh blow to these men who had given so much for their country, and they now complained bitterly.

One officer named Lewis Nicola did more than complain. He took action, circulating an anonymous letter among the men, putting "in writing what many officers were whispering behind the scenes: that the Continental Congress's erratic conduct of the war had exposed the weakness of all republics and the certain disaster that would befall postwar America unless Washington declared himself king."[34] It was a threat: if they did not receive their promised pay and pensions, the officers determined to seize control of the fledgling government. Of course he proposed that Washington should be their leader.

In reply, a horrified Washington told Nicola to "banish these thoughts from your Mind" and "denounced the scheme as 'big with the greatest mischiefs that can befall my Country.'"

The following March saw the arrival of what became known as the Newburgh Conspiracy. As Joseph Ellis writes in *His Excellency, George Washington*, "Scholars who have studied the Newburgh Conspiracy agree that it probably originated in Philadelphia within a group of congressmen, led by Robert Morris, who decided to use the threat of a military coup as a political weapon to gain passage of a revenue bill . . . and perhaps to expand the powers of the Confederation Congress over the states."[35]

An anonymous letter, which later became known as the Newburgh Address, made the rounds in Newburgh. Written by Major John Armstrong Jr., it contained not one but two threats: if Congress did not guarantee back pay and commutation, "the army would disband," even if the war continued (the peace treaty would not be signed until September 3, 1783). And if a peace treaty were signed, well then, the army would simply and absolutely refuse to dissolve. In effect, Armstrong was proposing tyranny and treason both.[36]

When Washington became aware of what was happening, the great man was horrified. And discovering that the leaders of the conspiracy planned to meet on March 11 to plot strategy, Washington stepped in. He "countermanded the order for a meeting [and] . . . scheduled a session for all officers on March 16."[37]

Washington then set about writing the speech of his life. Everything he believed in was at stake. For one thing, his hard-won reputation was in peril, but much more important, the very existence and future of America were threatened. If not for what he then said and did, all he had said and done up to that point might have been for naught: the newly birthed nation might well have been strangled in its cradle.

On March 16, just before noon, the officers were gathered in a newly built hall in Newburgh called the Temple, to await the start of the strategy session, which was to be chaired by General Horatio Gates. At twelve o'clock sharp, General Washington entered the room and strode to the podium. Silence fell over the room as Washington removed his speech from a pocket and began reading in his slow, quiet style.

First, he would rebuke them. "Gentlemen," he began, "by an anonymous summons, an attempt has been made to convene you together; how inconsistent with the rules of propriety, how unmilitary, and how subversive of all order and discipline."[38]

Many of the men present were angry with Washington for not doing enough, in their view, to secure their salaries and pensions. Washington reminded these men that he was one of them:

If my conduct heretofore has not evinced to you that I have been a faithful friend to the army, my declaration of it at this time would be equally unavailing and improper. But as I was among the first who embarked in the cause of our common country. As I have never left your side one moment, but when called from you on public duty. As I have been the constant companion and witness of your distresses, and not among the last to feel and acknowledge your merits. As I have ever considered my own military reputation as inseparably connected with that of the army. As my heart has ever expanded with joy, when I have heard its praises, and my indignation has arisen, when the mouth of detraction has been opened against it, it can scarcely be supposed, at this late stage of the war, that I am indifferent to its interests."[39]

Washington then got to the main point, referring to the—in his mind scandalous—letter that had been circulated:

But how are [these interests] to be promoted? The way is plain, says the anonymous addresser. If war continues, remove into the unsettled country . . . and leave an ungrateful country to defend itself. But who are they to defend? Our wives, our children, our farms, and other property which we leave behind us. Or, in this state of hostile separation, are we to take [our families] to perish in a wilderness, with hunger, cold, and nakedness?

If peace takes place, never sheathe your swords, says he, until you have obtained full and ample justice; this dreadful alternative, of either deserting our country in the extremist hour of her distress or turning our arms against it (which is the apparent object, unless Congress can be compelled into instant compliance), has something so shocking in it that humanity revolts at the idea. My God! What can this writer have in view, by recommending such measures? Can he be a friend to the army? Can he be a friend to this country? Rather, is he not an insidious foe?[40]

Washington then repeated what the soldiers had grown tired of hearing: that they should be patient as the Congress slowly sorted out how and when and how much to pay them. He also pointed out how far their mutiny would reach:

Why, then, should we distrust [the Congress]? And, in consequence of that distrust, adopt measures which may cast a shade over that glory which has been so justly acquired; and tarnish the reputation of an army which is celebrated through all Europe, for its fortitude and patriotism? And for what is this done? To bring the object we seek nearer? No! Most certainly, in my opinion, it will cast it at a greater distance.[41]

The old general then reminded his officers of what they had come to mean to each other:

For myself . . . a grateful sense of the confidence you have ever placed in me, a recollection of the cheerful assistance and prompt obedience I have experienced from you, under every vicissitude of fortune, and the sincere affection I feel for an army I have so long had the honor to command will oblige me to declare . . . that, in the attainment of complete justice for all your toils and dangers, and in the gratification of every wish, so far as may be done consistently with the great duty I owe my country and those powers we are bound to respect, you may freely command my services to the utmost of my abilities.[42]

Washington then gave what to many is the most moving part of his speech:

Let me entreat you, gentlemen, on your part, not to take any measures which, viewed in the calm light of reason, will lessen the dignity and sully the glory you have hitherto maintained. . . . Let me conjure you, in the name of our common country, as you value your own sacred honor, as you respect the rights of humanity, and as you regard the military and national character of America, to express your utmost horror and detestation of the man who wishes, under any specious pretenses, to overthrow the liberties of our country, and who wickedly attempts to open the floodgates of civil discord and deluge our rising empire in blood.[43]

He encouraged his men to look to the future—to imagine what generations yet unborn would think of them and what they had achieved:

By thus determining and thus acting, . . . you will give one more distinguished proof of unexampled patriotism and patient virtue, rising superior to the pressure of the most complicated sufferings. And you will, by the dignity of your conduct, afford occasion for posterity to say, when speaking of the glorious example you have exhibited to mankind, "Had this day been wanting, the world had never seen the last stage of perfection to which human nature is capable of attaining."[44]

Ironically, as magnificent and eloquent as these words are, it was not the words of Washington's speech that turned the tide and saved the American Experiment. Historians tell us that as Washington finished his speech, the room was perfectly silent.

But they differ in their opinions about precisely what happened next. Did Washington plan and rehearse his next move? Or was it a spontaneous act?

Announcing that he had something else to read to the men, Washington now reached into his uniform pocket and slowly pulled out a letter penned by a Virginia congressman. Washington unfolded it and began to read aloud, appearing to stumble over the words. Reaching into his waistcoat pocket, the general produced a pair of wire-rimmed spectacles. His men had never seen them before, although the fifty-one-year-old general had been using them as reading glasses for some time.

Washington apologized for the delay, saying, as he unfolded the spectacles and put them on: "Gentlemen, you must pardon me. I have grown gray in your service and now find myself growing blind."[45]

Somehow, these disarming, humble, and spontaneous words, spoken by the exceptional man standing before them, took everyone by surprise, and in an instant, the mood of the angry, battle-hardened men was utterly changed. Indeed, many of them wept openly as Washington read the letter and then quietly walked out of the room. The powerful temptation to crown Washington king or dictator and to wrest from Congress all control of the fledgling nation had been dealt a death blow—and the Nicola and Armstrong letters were cast upon the ash heap of history.

Who can imagine that the liberty of millions might depend on the character of one man? What was it that gave him the strength to do the right thing when the temptation to do something less noble must have been overwhelming?

In acting as he did that day—and on other occasions when the siren call of power might have overwhelmed a lesser man—Washington "demonstrated that he was as immune to the seductions of dictatorial power as he was to smallpox."[46]

Most of us can hardly fathom just how unusual Washington's decision was. In rejecting power, General Washington became the first famous military leader in the history of the world to win a war and then voluntarily step down instead of seizing and consolidating power. In fact, Washington's sworn enemy, George III of England, could scarcely believe his ears when he heard what Washington had decided to do. If the leader of the army that had defeated the most powerful military force on earth had indeed stepped down, as was being reported, George III declared that man would be "the greatest man in the world."[47]

Whatever else historians say about Washington, all celebrate his willingness to set aside the chance of being crowned King George I of America in favor of going back to being a Virginia farmer. Nor was this a decision he made hastily. Washington had made clear, in the very first year of the conflict, that he was determined not to win the war against King George III only to set himself up as a rival American tyrant once he had won. In a speech to New York leaders, Washington announced that, in becoming a soldier, he "did not lay aside the Citizen"—that is, he recognized civilian authority over the military.[48]

And yet Washington's decision still amazes.

As historian Joseph Ellis describes it,

> his trademark decision to surrender power as commander in chief and then president was not . . . a sign that he had conquered his ambitions, but rather that he fully realized that all ambitions were inherently insatiable and unconquerable. He knew himself well enough to resist the illusion that he transcended his human nature. Unlike Julius Caesar and Oliver Cromwell before him, and Napoleon, Lenin, and Mao after him, he understood that the

greater glory resided in posterity's judgment. If you aspire to live forever in the memory of future generations, you must demonstrate the ultimate self-confidence to leave the final judgment to them. And he did.[49]

◆ ◆ ◆

Of course the preceding events took place years before Washington became president. And yet most of us remember him principally as the first president of the United States. We forget that Washington wasn't simply the first president; he essentially invented the US presidency.

Before him, there was no such thing. He set the precedent for president, so to speak. Specifically, Washington had no model upon which to base such basic decisions as how the president should dress, whom he should meet, how he should make federal appointments, whether people should curtsy or bow to him, or even what he should be called (John Adams provoked much laughter by seriously suggesting that Washington be addressed as "His Elective Majesty" or "His Mightiness"). But let's be clear that what George Washington chose to do became the model for all who followed. Much of what he determined was adopted by virtually every other American president. Perhaps the most important of these decisions was when he refused to serve more than two four-year terms, another humble and selfless decision with incalculable ramifications for the nation's future. Washington also decided where every future president would live when he decided where the nation's capitol should be built.

In his first administration, Washington dealt with the massive debt the country had incurred fighting the war, including money borrowed from France, Spain, and Holland, which somehow had to be repaid. There were numerous conflicts with Indians who, armed by the British, continued to attack white settlements; the British, in defiance of the peace treaty, still kept troops on American soil. The first ten amendments to the Constitution were agreed on and passed into law.

Three more states—Vermont, Kentucky, and Tennessee—were added to the Union.

Actually, Washington wanted to retire at the end of his first term, longing to live at Mount Vernon with his wife and step-grandchildren. He had good reason to think he would be able to do this. As he had hoped and worked for, "a national government existed and was working," and he had "made the presidency into a potent and magisterial office. Already, many of the seemingly intractable economic tribulations of the war years and immediate postwar period had been rectified, and a bright future beckoned."[50]

But the president was pressured by others, including Thomas Jefferson, to stay in office for another term. Jefferson argued, "Your continuance at the head of affairs [is] of the [greatest] importance" because "the confidence of the whole union is centered in you." In addition, a second Washington term would keep "the Monarchial federalists," led by Alexander Hamilton, from "every argument which can be used to alarm & lead the people . . . into violence or secession. North & South will hang together, if they have you to hang on."[51]

Realizing that his country still needed him—especially with the French Revolution in Europe looming—Washington reluctantly agreed to serve a second term.

During the next four years, Washington, over objections by many who remembered how the French had come to America's aid during the war, kept out of the French Revolution, believing it was not in the best interests of the United States to get involved. His prescience in this decision is especially impressive. Washington also negotiated an end to the British practice of attacking and raiding American ships and taking American seamen prisoner. The owner of Mount Vernon, which was home to three hundred slaves, also oversaw the passage of the Fugitive Slave Law, which required all states, even those that had outlawed slavery, to return escaped slaves to their masters. To his sorrow, Washington saw the beginnings of political parties and partisan warfare.[52]

Washington, now sixty-four and exhausted by "those cares [of] which public responsibility is never exempt"[53] and by the increasing personal attacks, adamantly refused to consider a third term. After seeing John Adams inaugurated, Washington joyfully began riding the many miles of his farms again. He entertained the endless parade of guests who came to visit him and spend time with his family. Still, one thing nagged at him: What to do with his slaves?

Washington had wrestled with the slavery issue for much of his adult life, and in July 1799, he finally made an important decision. He rewrote his will, not only freeing his slaves but also ensuring that the young ones would be taught to read, write, and learn a trade, and that the old and infirm ones would be taken care of for the rest of their lives.

Five months later, on December 12, 1799, the sixty-seven-year-old general went out riding, as was his custom, to inspect his farms. The fact that it was storming meant little to him, and when he came in five hours later, he went to dinner in wet clothes. This was because he didn't want to keep his guest waiting. The next day he had the symptoms of a cold but insisted on going out nonetheless. That night he became seriously ill, and the next morning, doctors were summoned.

The medical care that Washington received horrifies us today. He was bled four times—five pints in all. To put this in perspective, that was more than 40 percent of the total amount of blood in his body. The doctors also "blistered" his neck with hot poultices and gave him laxatives. All of these treatments certainly made him weaker. Historians believe he was suffering from "a virulent bacterial infection of the epiglottis,"[54] but the antibiotics that could easily have treated it would not be discovered for more than a century.

Washington died on December 14, 1799, with his beloved Martha at his bedside. When the citizens of Alexandria learned of his passing, bells tolled unceasingly for four days and nights. In France, flags were lowered to half-mast. Out of respect, more than sixty British ships lowered their flags to half-mast as well, in honor of the man who had "out-generaled" them, as one British soldier put it during the war.[55]

◆ ◆ ◆

More than two hundred years after Washington's death, his willingness to relinquish power—twice—is the most remarkable thing that we remember about him. These refusals to seize power for himself were the greatest acts of one of history's greatest men.

Despite his human flaws, Washington was inescapably great. He was arguably the only man who could have overseen both the scuttling of the British and the rise of the American republic.

Historian John Ferling concludes that "merely by being there . . . Washington enabled the new nation to hang together and survive its terribly difficult infancy." He "ushered America toward modernity, fashioning the economic system that sustained growth and gradually made the United States a truly independent and powerful nation capable of maintaining its security."[56]

Historian Joseph Ellis writes that Washington led "the continental army to victory against the odds . . . thereby winning American independence." He secured "the Revolution by overseeing the establishment of a new nation-state during its most fragile and formative phase of development" and embodied "that elusive and still latent thing called 'the American people,' thereby providing the illusion of coherence to what was in fact a messy collage of regional and state allegiances."[57]

Ellis adds, "There was a consensus at the time, since confirmed for all time, that no one else could have performed these elemental tasks as well, and perhaps that no one could have performed them at all."[58]

Washington's successor, John Adams, would have agreed. Days after the general's demise, Adams said, "His example is now complete, and it will teach wisdom and virtue to magistrates, citizens and men, not only in the present age, but in future generations, as long as our history shall be read."[59]

It's a pity that most schoolchildren today think of Washington the way he's pictured on the dollar bill: as that slightly grumpy-looking old man. If I had my way, we'd replace those false images with portraits of the young, vibrant Washington, who can more easily be imagined dreaming big dreams, fighting significant battles, designing America's future—and then riding home to Mount Vernon, happy to have won his battles against power itself—the great temptation that can tempt mortal man. How grateful and how mightily blessed we are that he did.

TWO
William Wilberforce

1759–1833

lthough the first man in this book lived his whole life in America and the second man in this book lived his in England, both George Washington and William Wilberforce were roughly contemporaries and certainly knew of each other; both were tremendously famous during their lifetimes. You could even argue that Wilberforce was more famous. After his success in abolishing the slave trade and bringing "liberty to the captives,"[1] an Italian statesman described Wilberforce as "the Washington of humanity."[2]

One hundred and fifty years ago, men like Abraham Lincoln and Frederick Douglass spoke of him reverently as the great pioneer and father of the abolitionist movement. But in the last century or so, Wilberforce's name has faded significantly. Only in the last few years has this begun to change, due mainly to the 2007 movie *Amazing Grace*. That movie probably did more to popularize his story than anything else.

Many who saw the movie and perhaps read my biography (also titled *Amazing Grace*) couldn't believe they had never known of the great Wilberforce. One comment I have heard literally scores of times was: "After reading your book about this amazing man, I was ashamed not to have heard about him before!"

But how did *I* hear about Wilberforce?

Like so many others, I first heard about him from my friend Os Guinness. Anyone who didn't learn about Wilberforce from the movie probably heard of him through Os, who did more to keep Wilberforce's memory alive in the years before the film came out than anyone. It's likely the film never would have been made had not Os championed Wilberforce's story far and wide for so many years. But a great story is a great story, and when it's a true great story, it's hard to keep it to yourself. I'm tremendously grateful that Os didn't!

I had also heard about Wilberforce through my hero, Prison Fellowship founder Chuck Colson, the seventh man in this book. I worked for Chuck in the late nineties and learned that Prison Fellowship annually gave out a Wilberforce Award to someone for

> making a significant impact on the social ills of the day through personal effort, skill, and influence; for showing perseverance and selflessness in combating injustice, even to the point of willingness to sacrifice personal comfort, career, and reputation; for making a positive change in the values and character of society—"reforming manners"—through personal witness, example, and education; and for serving as an exemplary witness for Christ.[3]

Just from that glowing description, you couldn't help but wonder who Wilberforce was! But until I wrote my book about him, I really knew very little. I knew that Wilberforce was the member of Parliament who led the battle for the abolition of the slave trade. I knew his faith led him to take on this fight, and I knew that in 1807—after a nearly two-decades-long brutal campaign—he finally succeeded, earning the deserved encomia of the Western world. But that was about it. Actually, how I came to write about him—and learn much more about him—is a funny story.

It happened in 2005, when I wrote a book on apologetics, titled *Everything You Always Wanted to Know About God (but Were Afraid to Ask)*. In the beginning of one of those chapters—it was a chapter about the Bible—I briefly said that William Wilberforce was someone who took the Bible seriously, and as a result of this belief, he literally changed the world. Which is true.

One day in December of that year I found myself on CNN promoting my book. I was expecting the typical hardball questions, such as "How can God be all-powerful and good and yet allow so much horrible evil and suffering in the world?" and "How can an intelligent person believe in science and simultaneously swallow all the medieval nonsense that's in the Bible?" But I didn't get hardball questions. Instead, I got a softball question about William Wilberforce. I almost forgot I'd mentioned him in the book, but the next thing I knew I was talking about him to a national TV audience.

As a result of this interview, a publisher contacted me and asked if I would like to write a full-length biography about Wilberforce. A movie was in production (the aforementioned *Amazing Grace*), and it would make sense for someone to write a biography to appear at the time of the movie's release in February 2007. The movie and the book would commemorate the bicentennial of the 1807 abolition of the slave trade. Since I'd never written a biography before and had no ambition to write one, I had to think about it. But as it turned out, I was interested, and I spent the next year or so writing it.

In the course of my research for the book, I discovered that Wilberforce's leadership in the abolition movement was just a fraction of all that he did. His accomplishments were staggering, almost too many to believe. But I did the research, and the facts were there. I came to see what Os Guinness had long maintained, that Wilberforce was the most successful social reformer in the history of the world.

Wilberforce's story is so fascinating and so inspiring that I thought it important to recount the short version of it in this volume. His life stands as a shining example of what one human being—submitted to God's purposes for his life—is capable of doing.

◆ ◆ ◆

William Wilberforce was born in 1759, the only son of a very prosperous family of merchants in Hull, a large seaport city on the northeast coast of Great Britain. Billy, as he was called at a young age, was only nine when his father died. His mother also became terribly ill at that time, and most thought she would not survive. So she and Wilberforce's grandfather decided to send the boy to live with a very wealthy uncle and aunt at Wimbledon. That he should be raised in the environment of their elite social circle was of great importance to them.

It must be said that the cultural environment in England at that time was not at all Christian, except in the most superficial sense. The general falling away from serious Christianity in eighteenth-century England was due in part to the religious wars of the previous century, which had led to much bloodshed and misery. Most socially respectable people had moved away from any robust expression of the Christian faith and toward what we would today call Enlightenment rationalism or Deism. The "God" that was preached from many pulpits across England in those days was less Jehovah and Jesus, the personal God of Scripture, and more a vague, impersonal energy force.

Wilberforce's mother and grandfather followed this fashion, never taking their religious expression beyond church attendance and looking down on anyone who did otherwise. The Wesleyan revival meetings led by John and Charles Wesley and the evangelistic meetings of George Whitefield were mostly attended by common working-class people. So being "serious" about one's faith was thought of as perhaps acceptable for the lower classes, but to the Wilberforces and most elites, anyone who took God seriously was scorned as a *Methodist* or an *enthusiast.* These were the terms of derision in those days, much as *Holy Roller, Bible-thumper,* and *fundamentalist* have been used more recently.

So what happened to little William during the years he spent with his wealthy aunt and uncle would not have been at all approved by his mother and grandfather. That's because, quite unbeknownst to them, the extremely prosperous couple to whom they had sent little Billy were themselves devoted Methodists. In fact, they were so devoted to their evangelical Christian faith that they used their tremendous wealth to support many endeavors of the Methodist movement. George Whitefield himself often came to their grand home for weeks at a time to do what was called parlor preaching for their wealthy friends and neighbors. Although young William never met Whitefield, who died around that time, many other notable Methodist preachers visited, and the boy seems to have thrived in their company.

One of the most famous and frequent parlor preachers to visit their home was the colorful John Newton, the former slave trade captain who had been converted to the Christian faith and who eventually gave up the slave trade entirely. He became a well-known evangelical preacher, and with his friend, the English poet William Cowper, he wrote many hymns, among them "Amazing Grace." The young Wilberforce came to know Newton very well, almost thinking of him as a father, while Newton, for his part, thought of Wilberforce as a son.

But these happy times were not to last. When Wilberforce was about twelve, his grandfather and his mother were horrified to find out about the Methodism of the aunt and uncle. For them it was all a nightmare, almost worse than if the boy had been captured by Maori cannibals. After all, in their social circles Methodism was far more embarrassing. "If little Billy turns Methodist," his grandfather threatened, "he'll not see a penny of mine!"[4] Everything was at stake, so Wilberforce's mother raced the many miles from Hull to London to rescue her son from the clutches of these pious fanatics.

In the two-and-a-half years that he lived with them, Wilberforce had grown tremendously fond of his aunt and uncle, and they of him. He had come to embrace their faith as well. His sudden departure would be painful for both parties. When Aunt Hannah expressed her fears that Wilberforce might lose his faith if taken from them, Wilberforce's mother retorted, "If it be a work of grace [meaning if it's God's will] it cannot fail."[5] Her lack of seriousness about her own faith makes her statement interesting, to say the least, if not downright prophetic.

So against his wishes and those of his heartbroken aunt and uncle, Wilberforce was returned to life in Hull. His mother and grandfather now undertook to do everything possible to extinguish whatever spark of Methodism was in him, even refusing to allow him to attend their Church of England services, lest the mere liturgical reading of the Scriptures have any ill effects.

The twelve-year-old's faith was quite sincere, and he bravely clung to it with everything he had, even sending secret letters to his aunt and uncle by way of an obliging house servant. But after several years of the decidedly worldly environment, the ardor of his Methodism cooled. The endless parties and the fawning attentions paid to him as a soon-to-be extremely wealthy heir of his grandfather achieved their intended effect; by the time he was sent up to Cambridge, at age sixteen, William had backslid into a perfect picture of sophisticated worldliness. He had become every bit the insouciant young man of the world that his mother and grandfather had always hoped.

When he entered Cambridge, Wilberforce continued the lifestyle of parties and entertainments that he had enjoyed at Hull. Although he was never as terribly bold a sinner as some other students were, there is no question that he had walked away from the faith of his earlier years. He had also drunk the culturally acceptable waters of aloofness and skepticism toward anyone who took Christian faith seriously.

It was during his Cambridge days that he met William Pitt the Younger, who would play a significant role in his future life. Pitt's father, Pitt the Elder, was one of the most famous politicians and statesmen of that day, and he was training his brilliant son to follow in his footsteps. So Pitt the Younger would often travel from Cambridge to London to sit in the gallery of the House of Lords, where he would observe the parliamentary debates of the time and his new friend William Wilberforce often accompanied him.

Although his mother and grandfather expected Wilberforce to take over the family business, his creative, overactive mind and gay temperament were ill-suited to the life of a merchant. When he sat with Pitt watching the spectacular and engaging oratory on the floor of the House of Lords, it seemed that perhaps he should try his hand at politics instead. After all, Wilberforce was a renowned wit, adept at verbal jousting and oratory, talents that were crucial for someone hoping to enter the lists as a political candidate.

During their college years, Wilberforce and Pitt watched Parliament debate many subjects, most notably the fate of the American colonies. After all, it was the late 1770s, and the Revolution was under way. Of course King George III's government was of a mind to crush the colonial rebellion, whose military was led by a certain General Washington, but there were many dissenting voices in Parliament too, among them William Pitt the Elder. Those historic debates must have been intoxicating to the young Wilberforce, and it's no surprise that by the time he graduated Cambridge, he had indeed decided to try for a seat in Parliament.

Once he had made his decision, Wilberforce wasted no time, being elected to Parliament at the earliest allowable age, just two weeks after his twentieth birthday. William Pitt the Younger followed fast on his friend's heels, gaining a seat just a few months afterward. The two young Cambridge graduates soon rocketed through the political ranks to become some of the most powerful members of Parliament of that day.

With his winning personality and fine singing voice, Wilberforce also quickly became an extremely popular and well-known figure in London social circles. He became a member of five exclusive gentlemen's clubs, where he and his friends mixed with the celebrities of the day and were perpetually eating and drinking and singing and gambling until the wee hours of the morning.

Wilberforce's close friendship with Pitt continued, and in the year that both turned twenty-four, the pair and a third friend traveled to France for an extended holiday. Because Wilberforce and Pitt were already famous, all doors were opened to them. During that trip they visited the ill-fated couple, King Louis XVI and his queen, the young Marie Antoinette, who found Wilberforce especially charming. Wilberforce also met the Marquis de Lafayette, who had recently been a tremendous help to Washington and the American cause for freedom.

While he was with Lafayette, Wilberforce also met Benjamin Franklin, then the US minister to France. It's interesting to think that the seventy-seven-year-old Franklin, who was a lonely voice against slavery in the United States, should shake the hand of the twenty-four-year-old Wilberforce, who had yet to take up the battle in Great Britain. But Wilberforce's life was a catalog of meetings with the rich and famous. Many years later—in 1820—when Wilberforce was sixty-one and she only a toddler of eighteen months, Wilberforce had the honor of meeting the future Queen Victoria. It seemed that he met everyone and anyone of importance or celebrity in his lifetime.

At the age of twenty-four, Wilberforce was almost miraculously elected to an extremely significant seat in Parliament. It gave him a dramatic increase in visibility and political power. Around that same time—and also at the tender age of twenty-four—his friend Pitt was elected prime minister of the nation. Even in those days, such extreme youth in a prime minister was far from typical. One newspaper published a mocking verse:

> *A sight to make surrounding nations stare,*
> *A Kingdom entrusted to a school boy's care.*[6]

Pitt and Wilberforce proved up to the task, and Pitt knew that he never could have succeeded without his ally and friend Wilberforce beside him. The two friends were suddenly at the dizziest pinnacle of power and prestige. But it's what happened after this that makes Wilberforce one of the great men in this book of great men.

t all began in 1784—when Wilberforce decided to take a long vacation by traveling to the French and Italian Rivieras. His mother was ill again, and it was thought the trip to a warmer climate might help. She and a young cousin would travel in one coach, while Wilberforce and a companion-to-be-later-named would travel in Wilberforce's personal coach.

To travel there—twelve hundred miles as the crow flies—by the winding roads across the Alps would take many weeks, since the only means of travel was horse-drawn coach. Wilberforce had to choose his companion carefully. He first invited a certain Dr. Burgh to accompany him. Burgh was an Irish doctor whom he knew from York, but as it happened, he was unable to accept the invitation. Wilberforce surely didn't want to travel in his coach alone. The many hours could be passed far more profitably with a suitable travel companion. But whom to choose? Spending what would be hundreds of hours in such close quarters with the wrong companion could be difficult.

It was around this time that Wilberforce found himself at Scarborough, where he bumped into an old friend from childhood, Isaac Milner, who was ten years older than Wilberforce. Milner was the headmaster's brother at Wilberforce's grammar school and had worked at the school when Wilberforce was a student. But in the years since then he had become one of the most fascinating figures of that or any other era. Milner was now the Lucasian Professor at Cambridge, a post once held by Isaac Newton and more recently held by Stephen Hawking. It's no hyperbole to say that whoever holds that academic chair is one of the smartest men on the planet. But Milner was no mere egghead; he was famously jocular and celebrated as a teller of comic tales, often in the broad Yorkshire accent of his youth. He was even said to be the conversational heir to the eminent Dr. Johnson. Adding to his incomparable intellect and powers of entertainment was his nearly unbelievable size: Milner was a giant. Just how big he was is hard to say, but Wilberforce's friend Marianne Thornton once quipped that Milner "was the most enormous man it was ever my fate to see in a drawing room."[7]

So Milner accepted Wilberforce's invitation of an all-expenses-paid trip to the south of France, and the two of them were off. They must have made an odd couple. Wilberforce never grew above five-foot-three, and his chest measured a boyish thirty-three inches. Once, during a period of illness, his weight fell to seventy-six pounds. His green velvet waistcoat—today on display in the Hull museum that was his boyhood home—shows that this extraordinarily great man cut an exceptionally diminutive figure. Nonetheless he and Milner, for all their physical disparity, were well matched in intellect and wit, and their conversation across Europe and back must have sparkled beyond all reckoning.

But something happened during this long coach ride across Europe that would change the course of Wilberforce's life forever. At some point the subject of a certain evangelical pastor came up, and Wilberforce offhandedly remarked that the man in question "took things a bit too far."[8] Like everyone else in his circles, Wilberforce thought that anyone who took God very seriously went too far. But Milner did not agree, staunchly replying, "Not a bit."[9] Was Milner more serious about faith than Wilberforce had been led to believe? Evidently he was, and the conversation continued.

As the miles spooled past them, it became clear to Wilberforce that the effervescent genius with whom he now traveled was something of a closet Methodist. As far as Wilberforce was concerned, this was grievous news. Milner was in no way outwardly religious or off-puttingly aggressive in his views, but neither did he hold them lightly. In latter years Wilberforce admitted that, given his voguish antipathy for such thinking, if he had known beforehand he almost certainly would have chosen another traveling companion. But as the die was cast and they were far from home, Wilberforce was evidently obliged to engage the jumbo savant Milner in serious theological discussion.

To his credit, Wilberforce was intellectually honest, and he didn't shrink from robust debate. The back-and-forth between them continued across the Alps. Milner's intellect and vast learning on the subject were easily able to dispatch most of the objections to the faith that Wilberforce raised, and by the time their trip together had come to an end, Wilberforce was in the unpleasant and difficult spot of believing that he had been quite wrong in his previous views and that Milner had been right.

Wilberforce found to his significant distress that he had come to believe with his whole mind that what he had been sure was false was in fact true: the God of the Bible existed, Jesus existed in history and was the promised Messiah, and the Scriptures were not silly old myths but truth itself. For someone of his social standing and prestige, he was in a curious and uncomfortable position. What to do about it?

By the time Wilberforce returned to London, he was at a serious impasse. He knew that he could not reenter his former life professing the things he had now come to believe. He would be a laughingstock. Already his friends noticed that he was not showing his face at their parties or at any of the five gentlemen's social clubs he had once so hankered to join. For weeks on end, he remained in self-imposed isolation in his grand home, Lauriston House. What he was doing there his friends knew not, but it was soon bruited about that Mr. Wilberforce was "melancholy mad,"[10] which is to say, in a state of depression.

This observation was not far off the mark. Wilberforce simply had no idea how to reconcile what he had come to believe about God with his previous life. And his newfound and growing faith had become so central to him that he thought perhaps he would have to retreat from everything he knew and enter either a monastery or the priesthood. It was all tremendously inconvenient.

Years later, Wilberforce referred to this period of his conversion as

"The Great Change," and he characterized it as a gradual process that took between one and two years. Indeed, there were many changes in his life during this period. Some were superficial, such as the bold decision—executed in the space of a single day—to resign his memberships in all the exclusive gentlemen's clubs.

The activities in these clubs—gambling and drinking and other things inappropriate for a serious Christian—made leaving them a relatively easy decision for Wilberforce. But the question for him beyond this dramatic decision was much more complicated and difficult: Where exactly must one draw the line? Taking God seriously and leaving the so-called "world" meant resigning from these clubs, but what else must it mean? Would he have to leave the dirty world of politics also? On this point he wasn't clear, and for weeks and months the decision twisted in his mind.

It was while he was trying to answer this one question that Wilberforce made the fateful decision to visit his old friend John Newton.

Newton was then sixty and the famous rector of a church at Charles Square in Hoxton, an area of East London. It's unlikely that Newton and Wilberforce had had any contact since Wilberforce was taken away from his aunt and uncle at the age of twelve. Newton had doubtless followed the spectacular career of his brilliant young friend and been praying for him, but as Wilberforce had abandoned his childhood faith and had adopted the more secular attitude of his contemporaries, William might well have been embarrassed by his old sea-captain friend's unapologetic evangelicalism. Now that he had come to faith again, Wilberforce could think of no one better to speak with than this old friend.

But because Wilberforce was so famous, he feared being seen visiting Newton at his rectory, as this might tip people off to what was happening. And so Wilberforce preferred to visit Newton in secret, as Nicodemus had visited Jesus. Finally, one day in early December 1785, with much trepidation, he did so.

Newton was surely overjoyed to welcome his old friend and to know that he had come back to his Christian faith. But Wilberforce was less joyful in the meeting. In fact, he was painfully burdened about what course his life should take. Whether he must leave politics was the particular rub. We often talk today about how dirty politics is, but it was certainly much worse in Wilberforce's day.

But Newton, speaking perhaps prophetically, encouraged his young friend not to leave politics at all. Who knew—his reasoning went—but that Wilberforce had been prepared "for such a time as this"? Who knew but that God would use him mightily in the world of politics, where he was needed more than ever? It's hard to know what's more amazing, that Newton said such things or that Wilberforce accepted them; to remain as a serious Christian in that hostile secular climate was a brave thing indeed. But accept them he did.

And so Wilberforce vowed that he would take his faith into the world of politics and serve God there with his gifts.

◆ ◆ ◆

But how, exactly, should he go about it? How would it work out? To what major political objects should Wilberforce turn his attentions? That remained to be seen. But Wilberforce prayed about it and knew that God would lead him.

Less than two years after this historically important decision, Wilberforce wrote twenty words in his diary that would direct the course of the rest of his life. Those words, lived out during his lifetime, would have consequences so far-reaching that they would end in genuinely altering the course of Western civilization. "God Almighty," he wrote, "has set before me two Great Objects: the suppression of the Slave Trade and the Reformation of Manners."[11]

The meaning of these words must be explained. The first "Great Object" to which Wilberforce would dedicate himself mostly explains itself, and it's this first object for which he is principally known. Wilberforce had been aware of the abominable horror called the slave trade for many years. But he would count the cost before he threw himself wholeheartedly into anything, especially in a public way. He did not take lightly his reputation as a politician, and he needed to be sure he knew what he was getting into. He considered a number of issues that might make claims on his attention, and he wanted to be sure that God showed him which to choose.

During this time, a number of abolitionists—the famous Thomas Clarkson and Hannah More among them—realized that they must have a champion in Parliament. They needed a legislator as dedicated as they. And so they settled on Wilberforce and carefully approached him. Wilberforce was at first noncommittal, but in time he came to believe that God himself had called him to this noble task. In the brutal battle for abolition that lay ahead, he would need to know that it was God who had called him.

But what of the second "Great Object," the so-called "Reformation of Manners"? By this term Wilberforce did not mean what we think of when we hear the term *manners* today. He meant the reformation of morality or culture. In other words, he saw that all society was broken and in need of reform. British culture did not have a biblical worldview and did not regard human beings as being made in God's image and therefore worthy of dignity and respect. This unbiblical view led to every kind of evil. The terrible evil of the slave trade was only one—albeit the worst—of the social evils running rampant at that time.

So if the first Great Object was abolishing the slave trade, we might say that the second Great Object referred to addressing every other kind of abuse of human beings beyond the slave trade. Indeed, in Wilberforce's day, wherever one turned one saw abuse and decay and misery. So what Wilberforce called the "Reformation of Manners" was his larger attempt to attack that host of other social problems.

These social evils are worth listing, although it's hard to know just where to start. Child labor was one especially disturbing example. Poor children as young as five and six years old were often employed for ten- or twelve-hour days in horrendous and often dangerous conditions.

Then there was the wider problem of alcoholism, which contributed to almost all the other problems. It was an epidemic of proportions we can hardly imagine today. Everyone seemed to be addicted to alcohol, and there seemed to be nothing to help it. Members of the upper classes were perpetually drunk on claret—in fact, members of Parliament were often drunk during legislative sessions—and the lower classes were drunk on gin. The sexual trafficking of women was another staggering problem, one whose scope is almost inconceivable: fully 25 percent of all single women in London were prostitutes. And their average age was sixteen.[12]

For the entertainment of the perpetually drunken crowds, public displays of extreme animal cruelty such as bullbaiting and bearbaiting were very popular. When these grim spectacles were unavailable, public hangings, which were sometimes followed by ghastly public dissections, fit the bill. People were put to death for the smallest offenses, and the conditions of the prisons were unspeakable. Wherever Wilberforce looked, he saw a world untouched by the good news of Jesus Christ. People used and abused others in a perpetual downward spiral of misery and decay.

But Wilberforce knew that God had called him to do something about it. And since God had called him, he knew that he couldn't do it in his own strength. He would need God's help, and he would need the help of others.

Perhaps the most obvious sign of Wilberforce's conversion to the Christian faith was that it changed the way he looked at everything. Suddenly he saw what he was blind to before: that God was a God of justice and righteousness who would judge us for the way we treated others; that every single human being was made in God's image and therefore worthy of profound respect and kindness; that God was "no respecter of persons" and looked upon the rich and the poor equally.

Once Wilberforce had come to see that God was real and that God loved everyone, everything was different. Suddenly the idea of the slave trade and slavery itself seemed less an economic necessity than merely monstrous and wicked. Suddenly the idea that poor little children should be forced to work in awful conditions for long hours was disturbing and unacceptable. Suddenly the idea that those who had committed minor crimes should be thrown into filthy prisons, where they might die of any number of ailments for lack of treatment, was something that must be remedied. Suddenly the idea that women should sell their bodies so that they could feed themselves or feed their alcohol habit—or the alcohol habit of their pimps—could no longer stand.

For the first time in his life, Wilberforce saw the world through God's eyes. But he was living in a culture where almost no one saw things this way. So the task that lay ahead of him was impossible.

How would he do it?

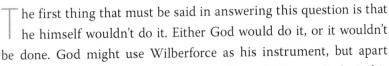

The first thing that must be said in answering this question is that he himself wouldn't do it. Either God would do it, or it wouldn't be done. God might use Wilberforce as his instrument, but apart from God, Wilberforce knew that he really could do very little. In his famous diary entry, Wilberforce wrote that it was "God Almighty" who had set the "two Great Objects" before him.

So Wilberforce didn't leap into the fray in his own strength. He first required a deep sense that God had called him to these things— else he would have been overwhelmed, and the many setbacks would have been a great discouragement. But because he knew that God had set these objects before him, he knew that the battle was God's battle, not his. All he had to do was to be obedient to what God was asking him to do and to know that God brings the victory.

Underscoring this point was a letter that Wilberforce received in 1791 from the great revivalist John Wesley, who was then eighty-seven years old and literally on his deathbed. The letter was written just days before Wesley died, and it seems to have been the last letter he ever wrote. Wesley knew of Wilberforce's heroic efforts against the slave trade, and he wrote to him on that very subject:

Dear Sir,

Unless the divine power has raised you up to be as Athanasius contra mundum [against the world], I see not how you can go through your glorious enterprise in opposing that execrable villainy, which is the scandal of religion, of England, and of human nature. Unless God has raised you up for this very thing, you will be worn out by the opposition of men and devils.

But if God be for you, who can be against you? Are all of them together stronger than God? O be not weary of well doing. Go on, in the name of God and in the power of His might, till even American slavery (the vilest that ever saw the sun) shall vanish away before it.

Reading this morning a tract wrote by a poor African, I was particularly struck by that circumstance, that a man who has a black skin, being wronged or outraged by a white man, can have no redress; it being a law in all our Colonies that the oath of a black against a white goes for nothing. What villainy is this!

That He who has guided you from youth up may continue to strengthen you in this and all things is the prayer of, dear sir,

Your affectionate servant,

John Wesley[13]

It's important to realize that the abominable racial views held by so many people at that time were not held by Wesley, Wilberforce, or most contemporary Methodists. The evangelical Christians of that time generally held God's perspective on this subject, and they stood in stark contrast to the views of people who were not Christians or to those who were cultural Christians and who perhaps attended church for social reasons, but who thought of the Methodists such as Wilberforce and Wesley as "taking things too far."

The main point in quoting Wesley's letter here is to show that this man who had battled a host of social evils for many decades knew better than anyone that without a full reliance on God, the battle could be brutal and all for naught. He felt compelled to warn young Wilberforce that to fight in one's own strength—even and perhaps especially in a noble and godly cause—was insanity; but to rely on God was to be assured of victory, even if one did not get to see it with one's own eyes.

In the battle against the slave trade that lay ahead, Wilberforce would experience a number of crushing defeats. And unless he really knew that God had called him to do what he was doing, it would be too much to bear.

The second point Wesley was making was that it was not merely a political or a cultural battle. It was a spiritual battle. When Wesley wrote, "you will be worn out by the opposition of men and devils," he was not using a colorful metaphor. He meant it literally.

To fight something as wicked as the slave trade was to go against an invisible demonic host. God has the power to fight them, but we do not. That spiritual reality lay behind the political reality, and Wesley wanted to ensure that Wilberforce understood that if he was to be successful in what lay ahead. Great men like Wilberforce and Wesley had the humility and the wisdom to know that whatever strengths they had—and they had many—they could not win without a total reliance on God. At its core, every battle worth fighting is a spiritual battle. Those men were able to succeed only because they humbled themselves and entrusted the battle to God.

But how does one do that?

This brings us to the second way that Wilberforce did what he did. The one-word answer is *prayer*. Wilberforce prayed and read the Scriptures every day, and he prayed with many others over these issues and concerns. He also memorized lots of Scripture. In my book *Amazing Grace*, I relate that he memorized the entirety of Psalm 119. That's hard to believe when you see how long it is, but it's true. Wilberforce would also sometimes walk the two and a half miles from Parliament to his home, and the second half of the walk took him through a portion of Hyde Park. Wilberforce had it timed so that if he began reciting Psalm 119 when he entered the park, he would be finished by the time he got home. It took about twenty minutes to recite the whole thing.

Third, Wilberforce was able to do all he did because of his reliance on a solid community of devout Christian brothers and sisters. Wilberforce was not what we today might call a "Lone Ranger" Christian, keeping his beliefs and prayers to himself. On the contrary, he thrived in the community of his fellow Christians and sought them out for strength and support and advice. The particular Christian community in which Wilberforce spent most of his time is famously known as the Clapham Circle because most of them lived in the London suburb of Clapham. Today Clapham is a bustling part of the city of London—just four miles from Westminster Abbey—but more than two hundred years ago it was a gloriously idyllic village, far from the world of Parliament.

Those who didn't share and were threatened by their religious views often derided members of the circle as the "Clapham Saints" or the "Clapham Sect." Even after he was very famous, most of fashionable society still felt that Wilberforce and his colleagues' religious ideas about things like helping the poor and abolishing slavery were embarrassing. These detractors would end up on the wrong side of history, but at the time, their secular notions were the norm.

It should be said that this Christian community known as the Clapham Circle did not happen by accident. On the contrary, it was the deliberate creation of Wilberforce's dear friend and relative John Thornton, who was extremely wealthy and who chose to buy a huge home at Clapham with twelve bedrooms for the express purpose of luring his friends to live there and share in the community. Thornton then expanded the home and bought others next door, hoping to get his brothers and sisters in Christ to be physically near each other so that they would benefit and be able to help each other in their various causes.

Those who didn't live at Clapham were always welcome to come and stay for weeks or even months at a time. In the mornings they would gather for breakfast and prayer, and whenever an important bill or issue was being worked on, they would pray together for strength and wisdom. Wilberforce would be the first to acknowledge that whatever he did, he did not do alone. First of all, God was the one behind every battle and every victory; and second, the living community of Clapham believers was involved on all levels.

've said that the battles Wilberforce fought were at their core spiritual battles, and this is true of every battle worth fighting. But even once we see that there is a spiritual battle at the center of every battle, we may sometimes think that the main battle in this world is a political one. If only we can elect so-and-so, or if only we can get this law passed or that law repealed, all problems will be solved. But Wilberforce was effective over the course of his lifetime because even though he was a tremendously successful politician, he realized that some battles must be fought in the cultural sphere too.

The battle against the slave trade was largely won when a bill passed both houses of Parliament in 1807, but Wilberforce knew that in order to get the votes he needed to win that particular political battle, he would have to change the hearts and minds of people first—and that was very much a cultural battle. This realization prompted Wilberforce to say that part of his strategy in fighting many of these social evils was to "make goodness fashionable."[14]

He was a legislator and a politician, but he was also an important cultural figure with many influential friends; he had the ability to influence how people thought about things, and he knew that this would have a wide-ranging effect. At the time, goodness was not fashionable at all. To really change things, Wilberforce would have to change the cultural fashions, especially among the elites.

To see one vivid example of just how deeply bad behavior was in vogue, we must only consider the Prince of Wales, a notorious rake who eventually would become King George IV. His father, George III, may have been powerfully misguided in his dealings with the American colonies, but he was an essentially good man who loved his wife and his many children, often reading the Bible to his daughters in the evenings. But his eldest son was quite the opposite. In fact, the Prince of Wales was widely celebrated for having had seven thousand sexual conquests. This and his other myriad indiscretions were well known. If a leading figure in the land is behaving in this fashion, it sets a tone and an example that are powerfully counterproductive to a healthy culture.

Wilberforce used the influence and cultural position that he had to point in another direction. For example, Wilberforce and his wife had six children, and Wilberforce spent every Sunday at home with his family, playing with the children inside and outside their home in Clapham. To us, this behavior sounds rather normal, but in his day it was not the fashion for fathers to spend much time with their children or to observe the Lord's Day as Wilberforce did. He sent a powerful cultural message that family was important, and being a good father and family man meant spending quality time with one's family.

Making goodness fashionable wasn't just setting an example against badness. What Wilberforce wanted to do—and largely succeeded in doing—was to make "doing good" fashionable. It's hard to believe that before Wilberforce the very idea of helping those less fortunate was practically nonexistent. If someone was suffering, the general consensus was that he had brought his difficulties upon himself and he must deal with the consequences of his behavior.

But Wilberforce dared to dream about changing this mind-set. What if people who had money and power and influence would be willing to use those things to do good for their fellow men? What if he could bring a biblical worldview into the culture?

The biblical idea first mentioned in Genesis 12 that we are "blessed to be a blessing" was not at all considered, much less practiced, at that time. Thanks in large part to Wilberforce, most of the Western world today believes that those who are fortunate have some obligation to help those who are less fortunate. But for Wilberforce's contemporaries this idea was quite foreign. Wealthy persons believed they had wealth because God was on their side and they were consequently "blessed." Conversely, they believed that those who did not have wealth deserved their difficulties and were being judged by God. So to help them would be to go against God's purposes. Of course this view is the antithesis of God's view, but it was tremendously widespread. This is really more an Eastern Karmic idea of why people suffer and struggle. In India, a Brahmin would never dream of helping an Untouchable, because their misery was thought to be due to their bad Karma; they deserved their misfortune. One's wealth was thought to be due to one's good Karma, and was therefore deserved. Therefore to help the poor would be to thwart the "divine" plan.

Dramatic as it sounds, Wilberforce's tremendous efforts to change this mind-set over the course of many decades can rightly be seen as one of the most significant accomplishments in history. It was a radical idea, taken by one man from the Gospels into mainstream British culture at a time when the British Empire was huge and tremendously influential. Consequently, these biblical ideas were spread throughout the world, especially throughout Western Europe and the new United States of America.

We in the West have been living with them ever since then, and we've gotten so used to thinking this way that we can hardly imagine a world without them. We assume such ideas were always the norm, but the reality is precisely the opposite. Until Wilberforce and his friends were able to change the culture of elite London and England, these ideas of helping the poor and those less fortunate were essentially unknown.

◆ ◆ ◆

As I have traveled and spoken about Wilberforce over these last years, people have often asked me how Wilberforce did what he did. Although I've noted some of how he did what he did already, it's important to say that Wilberforce wasn't just "religious" but actually had a personal relationship with God. He seems to have been motivated by love—love of God and the love of his fellow man—more than by a simple sense of right and wrong or justice and injustice. This is probably the single most important factor in what he was able to do.

Wilberforce knew the God of the universe as a loving Person who had intervened in his life, so he was filled with gratitude to God for being able to see what he saw and was slow to condemn those who didn't yet see things as he did. Most people, therefore, regarded his humility as authentic.

First of all, Wilberforce was willing to share the credit for all that he did with others, and he knew that he was just one of many working for reform in all these areas. He worked with many friends who were theologically and politically on the same page as he was, most of them in the Clapham Circle.

But second—and even more dramatic—was Wilberforce's ability to work with people with whom he disagreed. For example, he worked with Charles James Fox on the abolition issue, even though Fox was his opponent in many political battles. Fox was also notoriously dissolute and a close friend of the Prince of Wales, but Wilberforce understood that he himself had been saved by grace, and he was not about to pretend to have moral superiority because he disapproved of another's moral or political views. He would show others grace as he had been shown grace, and he would work with them, if possible, toward some common and noble purpose, such as abolishing the slave trade. Wilberforce was clear about what he believed, but he never made agreeing with him on everything a condition of working together. He simply cared about the slaves and about the poor too much for that.

Taking this idea one step further, Wilberforce loved his enemies. He didn't grandstand and fulminate at those who were wrong, even if the subject was the horror of the slave trade. He included himself in the group of those who were guilty. When he gave his maiden speech on abolition on the floor of Parliament, he said, "We have all been guilty."[15] And of course that was true. Wilberforce understood the profoundly important concept that we are all sinners and all fall short of the glory of God. He hated the sin but loved the sinner, and he never demonized his opponents. He fought against them valiantly but always with grace, knowing that he had been part of the problem at one time, too, and knowing that if it weren't for the grace of God, he would still be a part of the problem.

Wilberforce's graciousness in the midst of the battle against the slave trade did a lot to persuade those who were on the fence instead of putting them off and pushing them away. He knew that God had commanded him to love his enemies. It wasn't an option. So he would fight his opponents and try to win, but he would do it God's way, showing love and grace even as he fought with tremendous passion.

His profoundly Christian attitude even helped England beyond the cause of abolition. England was leaning toward the same kind of revolution that was occurring in France. But Wilberforce's statesmanship and measured grace set a tone of such civility that England was somehow able to avoid the bloodbath and misery that took place across the Channel in France.

In 1807, after eighteen years of heartbreaking effort and many near misses, Wilberforce's dream came true. The much-worked-toward, much-prayed-for dream of the abolition of the slave trade became a reality. He was then forty-eight years old. He had contended with life-threatening illnesses over the years, and he continued to deal with them until the end of his life. Furthermore, opponents of abolition threatened his life numerous times. But the slave trade was finally outlawed.

The battle was not over. Wilberforce spent the remainder of his life working to ensure that the promise of abolition was fulfilled. Enforcement in England and its empire was difficult, since what was illegal remained possible (and highly profitable) for those willing to break the laws. For generations, the British Royal Navy scoured the oceans, searching for and intercepting ships that carried their illegal human cargo.

Also, Wilberforce set out to persuade the other major powers of the world—France, Spain, and Russia, especially—to adopt abolition. He knew that unless these nations and the United States were also determined to root out this evil, his efforts had been mostly for naught. So even after the glorious victory of 1807, the abolitionist battle continued on many fronts.

Only after 1808, when the slave trade was officially ended, did Wilberforce see that abolishing the slave trade alone was not enough. He and others had perhaps naively hoped that by abolishing the trade, slavery would eventually die out. But they quickly realized that was not the case and earnestly set themselves to abolishing slavery altogether. This was itself a decades-long battle. At last, in 1833, just three days before Wilberforce's death, he received a visitor who brought extraordinary news. A young member of the House of Commons told him that earlier that day Parliament had voted to outlaw slavery. Hearing this magnificent news on what turned out to be his last day of consciousness was the fitting coda to a spectacular life, one lived out in obedience to the God who had created him.

The world that Wilberforce left behind was dramatically different from the one he had entered seventy-three years earlier. Not only had the slave trade and then slavery itself been abolished, but the once foreign and strange idea that one should help those less fortunate had taken hold. As a result, much else would change, and those changes have been with the West ever since.

How God used William Wilberforce to change the world is almost unbelievable. One man who gave his talents and time and energies to God's purposes was able to do so much. But we who admire him shouldn't compare ourselves to him directly. We should rather ask ourselves: Am I using what God has given me for his purposes? Do I have a relationship with him so that I know he is leading me? Am I obeying him in all areas of my life—or trying to do so—so that I can know I am in a real relationship with him?

It was in his honestly asking and answering these few questions that lay at the heart of the greatness of the great William Wilberforce.

THREE
Eric Liddell

1902–45

When I was a student at Yale in the 1980s, a group of friends and I went to see the British film *Chariots of Fire*. It was a box office blockbuster, and everyone was talking about it. In fact it would go on to win the Academy Award for Best Picture, and it seemed that you couldn't go anywhere without hearing the music from the sound track. The movie was one of those cultural milestones that takes over the culture for a while, even to the point of inspiring spoofs and parodies. But this film was worth all the hoopla; it's surely one of the most inspiring, well-written, and gorgeously filmed movies ever made.

To all of us watching it in that theater in New Haven, Connecticut, the story and its hero were brand new. We certainly had never heard of the main figure in the film, Eric Liddell, the Scottish runner who electrified the world by winning the 400-meter race during the 1924 Paris Olympics. And we had never seen a movie about someone whose faith was at the center of his life. But what made Liddell's story so inspiring was not just that he won an Olympic gold medal, but that he won it after refusing to run his best event, the 100 meter. And that was because those heats took place on a Sunday—"the Lord's Day," as he put it.

Even though I wasn't a particularly serious Christian at the time, I found *Chariots of Fire* deeply inspiring. And a few years after graduating from Yale—when I came to faith in a serious way—I recalled the story of Liddell, and I wanted to learn more about him and about the film.

I discovered that although the makers of the movie had taken some liberties with the facts (what filmmaker doesn't?), the gist of the story was accurate. More important, I realized the amazing truth that had Eric Liddell run that 100-meter race, as he was urged to do, he would be largely forgotten today outside of Scotland. If you don't believe me, quick, how many other gold medal winners from the 1924 Olympics can you name? Okay, what about 1928? See?

So Liddell is remembered today for one reason. He was willing to make an almost impossible sacrifice: not only the greatest prize in sports but also the chance to bring honor to his beloved country—not to mention fame, fortune, and glory to himself.

What even Eric Liddell did not know until after the 100-meter race was won by Harold Abrahams was that the God who endowed the young Scot with outstanding athletic ability would bring glory to himself through Liddell's refusal to use these gifts at the very moment the world's eyes were on him.

But there's still so much more to his story. If you know little of Liddell beyond what's in the film—that he won an Olympic gold medal and died in China while serving there as a missionary—I'm confident that you'll appreciate the rest of his amazing story.

◆ ◆ ◆

Eric Henry Liddell was born on January 16, 1902, in Tientsin, China, where his parents, James and Mary Liddell, were missionaries. The blond, blue-eyed boy was nearly two years younger than his brother, Robert, born in August 1900 in Shanghai. A sister, Janet (Jenny), joined the family in 1903.

The turn of the twentieth century was a decidedly dangerous time to be a missionary in China. The Boxer Rebellion (1898–1901) was a recent, vivid, and disturbing memory in which nationalist Chinese militants purposed to eliminate all foreign influence, in the process murdering thousands of Chinese Christians and hundreds of Westerners, including missionaries and their families. Warlords competed for power over villages and towns, and bandits kidnapped the well-to-do, holding them for ransom. But the Liddells knew God had called them to China; they would remain there despite the dangers and leave the consequences in the Lord's hands.

Before Eric's first birthday, his parents left Tientsin for Siaochang, where they lived in a newly built house within the compound of the London Missionary Society. There a Chinese nanny, or *amah*, looked after the three Liddell children. Eric was a sickly child, whose mother nursed him through many an illness, but when he was healthy, he and his siblings enjoyed life in the compound. The Liddells were very pious and serious about God, but they also knew how to have fun. At one point, they even allowed the children to adopt a family of goats.

When Eric was five, his parents took the family back to Croftamie, Scotland, on furlough. This was the children's first sight of their family's native land, whose green mountains and sparkling lochs were very different from their dry and dusty Chinese home. Eric and his brother, Robert, explored the village, picked blackberries, and enjoyed being spoiled by the many Liddell relatives who lived there.

At the end of the summer of 1907, just before he and his wife were planning to return to China, James Liddell enrolled his sons in the School for the Sons of Missionaries (later called Eltham College) just outside London. Missionary parents routinely left their children behind for seven years so that they could pursue their educations. The boys' mother, Mary, intended to travel back to China with her husband and young daughter; but just before it was time to go, she changed her mind. She could not bear the thought of leaving her two young sons for so long, so she decided to stay in Great Britain for a year to make sure her boys would be happy at the school, and she moved with Jenny to a house near the campus.

During their years at Eltham, Robert and Eric studied mathematics, languages, science, English, Latin, the classics, geography, and the Scriptures. Outside the classroom, they played touch rugger and looked after a collection of pet birds and lizards. During debates with other boys, Eric was usually quiet, preferring to think about the answers he was hearing rather than entering into the discussions themselves.

In early 1913, the boys received a letter from their mother telling them of the arrival of a third brother—Ernest—in December 1912. When Mary Liddell's ill health and need for surgery brought the Liddells back from China a year earlier than they had planned, Rob and Eric were overjoyed to see their family again.

As Europe was hurtling toward the First World War, both Robert and Eric—then fourteen and twelve, respectively—began excelling in school sports. They played cricket and rugby, and on a school sports day, in the under-thirteen age classification, Eric placed first in the high jump, long jump, and 100-yard dash.

Robert was outgoing and gregarious, joining the debate club and seeking leadership positions. By contrast, Eric grew into a shy, quiet teenager who loved mathematics and science—especially chemistry—and sports.

But his natural diffidence did not stop him from competing ferociously on the playing fields. He had been gifted with a staggering natural talent. In 1918, when he was sixteen, Eric competed in the school championships and took everyone's breath away by placing first in three events: the long jump, the quarter-mile, and the 100-yard dash (tying the school record of 10.8 seconds). Eric also took second place in the hurdle race, the cross-country run, and the high jump. It was a phenomenal performance.

In his senior year, Eric was awarded the coveted Blackheath Cup (an honor given to the best all-around sportsman) and was named the captain of the school's rugby team. Both awards showed that Eric was not just gifted athletically: the gentle young man was also very popular with his classmates.

After Eric's graduation in 1920, he and Robert were again reunited with their mother, sister, and brother Ernest, who had returned to Scotland for another furlough. In February 1921, Eric entered the University of Edinburgh, where he studied physics and chemistry. Amazingly, given his heavy academic schedule, taking part in his beloved sports did not even occur to Eric at this time. But within a few weeks, a fellow classmate wheedled him into participating in the University Athletic Sports Day in late May.

On the day of the competition, Eric's time of 10.4 seconds in the 100-yard dash—which was not his best—won him the race. More important, it won him a place on the university's track team, which would compete against other Scottish schools.

◆ ◆ ◆

If you've seen *Chariots of Fire*, you probably remember the controversy surrounding the decision by Cambridge runner Harold Abrahams to hire a professional trainer. But Eric Liddell had a personal trainer, too, albeit one who worked with him on a volunteer basis. This was to prevent any possibility of Liddell's putting his amateur standing in jeopardy, thus running afoul of the Olympic rules. Under the canny tutelage of Tommy McKerchar, Eric won race after race, competing in the 100- and 220-yard events and quickly attracting the attention of the press, which predicted that a new Olympic contender might be at hand. The public took note of the unusually gracious behavior of the young Scot. Before each race, he always shook hands with his competitors and wished them the best, often lending them his trowel in order to dig their starting blocks, something all sprinters were required to do in those days.

The film accurately captures Eric Liddell's peculiar running style: arms flailing like windmills and knees pumping high. As he approached the finish line, Eric would throw his head back and open his mouth wide. Odd and unorthodox as this style was, McKerchar apparently did not attempt to get Eric to run in a more conventional manner. It was almost as if in throwing his head back, Eric had to rely totally on God to direct him to the finish line, since he couldn't see it himself.

In 1921 Eric joined brother Rob on Edinburgh's rugby team, exhibiting the same ferocious desire to win that he displayed in his running. Two years in a row he was honored to be selected for the Scottish International Team. But in rugby the chances of injury were considerable, so after his second year of play, Eric gave it up and chose to focus on running. Word of his terrific speed eventually earned Liddell the nickname of "The Flying Scotsman," after the well-known express train that connected Edinburgh to London, making the nearly four-hundred-mile journey in just over eight hours.

◆ ◆ ◆

In April 1923, Eric's growing fame led to the first invitation to speak publicly about his faith. It came from the Glasgow Students' Evangelistic Union, which was engaged, with little success, in an evangelistic rally in a hardscrabble coal-mining town outside Edinburgh. But what if Scotland's fastest sprinter were among the speakers? Perhaps then the men would come and listen. So one of the group's founders, divinity student David Patrick Thomson, agreed to ask Liddell. He traveled all the way to Edinburgh and knocked on the door of the house that Eric shared with his older brother. Eric himself answered, and Thomson put the question to him. Eric thought about it for a few moments and then agreed to do it.

But Eric hated public speaking, and no sooner had he given his assent than he began to regret it. The very next morning he received a letter from his sister, Jenny. At the end, she quoted Isaiah 41:10 (KJV): "Fear thou not; for I am with thee: be not dismayed; for I am thy God: I will strengthen thee; yea, I will help thee; yea, I will uphold thee with the right hand of my righteousness."

Eric felt that those words were God's way of speaking directly to him. Some time later, he said that "those words helped me make my decision, and since then, I have endeavored to do the work of the Master."[1]

When Eric arrived at the meeting, he found some eighty coal miners waiting to hear him. Eric spoke quietly about his faith in Christ, "of what God meant to him," and

> the strength he felt within himself from the sure knowledge of God's love and support. Of how he never questioned anything that happened either to himself or to others. He didn't need explanations from God. He simply believed in Him and accepted whatever came.[2]

Decades later, Eric's daughter Patricia noted, "He felt, 'now who's going to come and listen?' But those times where he went speaking, huge crowds [showed up]."[3] Eric "brought in people who might not have been interested in religion as such, but more into sports: let's see what this sports hero has to say."[4]

Few who heard him speak would have claimed that Eric was a great speaker. His natural shyness kept him from being passionate in his oratory, but somehow his sincerity and self-deprecating humor came through. They certainly did that day. Many of the miners who had come to hear him were deeply moved.

News spread rapidly that the Flying Scotsman had spoken publicly about his faith. Eric soon joined the evangelism group and began speaking with them in town after town, fitting in engagements during school holidays. It gave him great joy to know that God could use his athletic prowess in this way. Years before, Eric had committed himself to serving God in some way, but it seemed he had few talents other than an ability to run like the wind. His heart's desire was to glorify God, and he didn't think that being able to run fast—even as fast as he could run, which was very fast indeed—was of any eternal purpose. Why had God given him this world-class talent? What was the point?

But now he began to see the point, and he was suddenly tremendously grateful for his rare gift.

As he later put it,

> My whole life had been one of keeping out of public duties, but the leading of Christ seemed now to be in the opposite direction, and I shrank from going forward. At this time I finally decided to put it all on Christ—after all if He called me to do it, then He would have to supply the necessary power. In going forward the power was given me.[5]

At this time, Eric became very interested in what came to be known as the Oxford Group—men from Oxford University who urged Christians to surrender completely to God each day and live by the Four Absolutes: absolute honesty, absolute purity, absolute unselfishness, and absolute love. They also urged people to have a daily "quiet time," in which they would read a portion of the Scriptures, pray, and listen quietly for God's leading. Eric would do this for the rest of his life, even during the dark days when he lived in an internment camp in occupied China.

I f you've seen the movie, you will probably remember that one of the most unforgettable and dramatic scenes in *Chariots of Fire* involves a quarter-mile race in which Eric is accidentally knocked down by a competitor but against all human odds manages to win anyway. The remarkable event really did happen in July 1923 at Stoke-on-Trent at a so-called Triangular Contest track meet between Scotland, England, and Ireland. Literally right out of the blocks—near the very start of the race—Eric was badly knocked down, and in a quarter-mile race at such a high level of competition, fractions of a second determine the winner. Anyone knocked down is quite simply out of contention. But such accidents are unavoidable in the intense rough-and-tumble crowding of such races.

In this instance, however, despite the fact that he was twenty yards behind, Eric leaped back to the track and madly gave pursuit. That he was twenty yards behind made the attempt to rejoin the relatively short race seem utterly absurd. Nonetheless, Liddell ran at such an astonishing pace that the spectators were goggle-eyed and on their feet, rapt by the unfolding scene before them. Accelerating from far behind, Liddell managed to catch and pass one runner and then another until impossibly, he finally overtook the leader and won the race, at last collapsing onto the cinder track. It was an athletic performance for the ages, and no one who was there would ever forget it.

In 2012, *New York Times* writer David Brooks wrote a column claiming that the charitable aspect of the Christian faith was at odds with the killer instinct needed to win in athletic competition, so that serious faith was a hindrance to victory.[6] But Eric Liddell is the classic example of someone whose faith was not only *not* at odds with the will to win, but also, indeed and on the contrary, was a tremendous boon to it. His competitive instinct, as evinced in this one race, was simply unparalleled. Because he desired to use his athletic gifts to glorify God and because he knew that his winning gave him an opportunity to speak about God to men who otherwise might not be at all interested in the subject, running and winning had an eternal purpose. Because he was not merely running for himself, Liddell was able to summon powers that sometimes seemed miraculous, even to avowed skeptics.

After that famous race, when some of the astonished onlookers asked him how he had managed to win, Liddell again seized the opportunity to publicly glorify God. He reportedly replied, "The first half I ran as fast as I could. The second half I ran faster with God's help."[7]

Although the movie *Chariots of Fire* showed us this dramatic incident, it never told us what happened as a result: Eric had pushed himself so hard to win that he damaged muscle tissue and had severe headaches for days afterward. Those few seconds of superhuman exertion on the track took so much out of him that he didn't even place at a 100-meter race two weeks later, and the 100 was his signature event, one in which he had recently set a record. Indeed, as it turned out, Eric Liddell had given so much in that single performance that he didn't win another race again for the rest of that summer. The 1924 Paris Olympics were just one year away, but even though he did not win any races after that memorable day in Stoke-on-Trent, Liddell was still considered a probable Olympic contender.

To heighten the dramatic effect, *Chariots of Fire* suggests that Eric did not receive the news that the heats for the 100-meter race—his best event—would take place on a Sunday until he was boarding the ship that carried the British team to the Paris Games. But in reality, Eric learned about this in the fall of 1923. This was when, as a prospective Olympic contender, he received the schedule of events from the British Olympic Association.

Still, while deeply regretting that he would not be able to run, Eric did not hesitate making and abiding by his decision. As far as he was concerned, Sunday was the Lord's Day—not a day for playing games— even the Olympic Games. Instead, it was a day for rest and worship. Eric took the Lord's command seriously, that we are to observe the Sabbath day and keep it holy. *Holy* simply means "separated unto God." As he saw it, running in the Olympics on that day was out of the question, and Eric could not compromise on what he believed God had commanded.

While the real Eric Liddell was not confronted by the Prince of Wales and the British Olympic Committee for his decision, as we see depicted in the movie, the scene nonetheless accurately represents the attitude of the British Olympic Committee toward Eric's decision: they were flabbergasted and outraged. And they were not about to let the misguided fanaticism and arrogance of this overly religious young man ruin Scotland's chances for national glory! They would use any means necessary to get this annoyingly headstrong man to run.

First, they tried to convince Liddell that there was no real problem with running on Sunday; after all, his heat wouldn't take place until the afternoon, leaving him more than enough time to attend church services in the morning. Eric didn't buy it. Nor did he buy the argument that he could worship God in the morning and run to God's glory in the afternoon. When, in frustration, a committee member pointed out that the Continental Sabbath lasted only until noon, Eric testily responded, "Mine lasts all day."[8]

When the British Olympic Committee realized that Eric was an immovable object and would not budge, they tried another tack: they would try to budge the International Olympic Committee. They lodged an official appeal to have the heats for the 100-meter race moved to another day in order to accommodate any participants whose religious beliefs prevented them from taking part on the Sabbath. This was a terribly sporting effort on their part: the appeal was denied nonetheless.

The British Olympic Committee was hardly alone in being upset with Liddell's decision not to run in his best event, the one in which he was likely to bring glory to Scotland. When news of his decision became public, many Scots—excited over the chance of Scotland winning its first-ever Olympic gold medal—were aghast at his decision. They felt he had betrayed them. To bow out of the 100 meter at this point was taking things too far. What was it but insanity? As for his chances in the 400 meter, Liddell was a world-class sprinter, not a world-class quarter-miler. It was all an awful mess, but everyone assumed the young man eventually would come to his senses.

But Eric had made up his mind. More important, he felt that he had God's mind on the subject, and that was all that mattered. Eric would obey God, and God would sort out the details of who won what medal. Even if he faced a lifetime of calumny and ignominy for his decision, his desire was to glorify God and to obey God, and the results in these Olympics and in his future life were in God's hands.

So in the end—with just six months to go before the Paris Games—Eric made his decision irrevocable and began training not for the 100-meter race but for the 400-meter event. The 400 is not merely longer than the 100; it is a middle-distance race and requires a completely different strategy. On June 20 of that year, Liddell took part in the Amateur Athletic Association Championships in London. This competition would determine whether he would be tapped for Britain's Olympic Team. Many had their doubts, but the fleet-footed Scotsman nailed his place on the team by finishing second in the 220 and by winning the 440.

◆ ◆ ◆

On Saturday, July 5—roughly two weeks later—the grand opening ceremonies for the 1924 Olympics were held. Two thousand competitors from around the world entered Colombes Stadium in Paris. They watched and listened as the Olympic flag was raised, cannons roared, and thousands of pigeons were released. Eric Liddell was there, snappily dressed in a blue blazer, white flannel pants, and a straw boater, as was the rest of the British team.

The following day—Sunday, July 6—the heats for the 100-meter race were held. Who can imagine what went through Eric's mind that day? But we know what he did. Eric first attended church and then joined his teammates and the Prince of Wales at a ceremony at the Tomb of the Unknown Soldier honoring those who had died in the First World War. Because feelings still ran high over the terrible costs of that war, Germany was not allowed to compete in the Games that year.

The final for the 100 meter was held the next day, Monday, July 7. Eric sat in the stadium watching while his teammate Harold Abrahams, far below on the track, waited tensely for the sound of the starting pistol. When the pistol fired, the runners burst forth, and 10.6 seconds later, Abrahams broke the tape, just ahead of the American, Jackson Scholz. Liddell joined enthusiastically in the roar of delight from British fans, celebrating Great Britain's first-ever win in this event.

The heats for Liddell's two events took place over the next four days. On Wednesday, July 9, Liddell, Abrahams, and four others, including Jackson Scholz, lined up for the final in the 200 meter. British onlookers were hoping for a win by Abrahams. But 21.6 seconds later, it was Scholz who crossed the finish line first, with his teammate Charley Paddock taking silver a tenth of a second later. Liddell, finishing a tenth of a second after Paddock, took home the bronze medal, Scotland's first ever. But this achievement was mostly overlooked in the shock and disappointment over Abrahams's placing not first in this race but dead last.

The 400-meter finals were held the very next day—Thursday, July 10. The overwhelming and sensible view that Eric would not win this event was powerfully confirmed when the American Horatio Fitch shattered the world record in the 400-meter semifinal heat early in the day, with a time of 47.8. Liddell, running in the second heat, managed to finish first, but his time was 48.2—two-fifths of a second behind Fitch's.

And there was more bad news for Liddell. When the six finalists drew lanes for the 400-meter final that evening, Eric drew the outside lane, widely considered the worst possible position. This was because the runner in the outermost lane started the race far in front of his opponents, unable to see them and compare his progress to theirs. Given that this race was hardly his best event, given that Fitch had outperformed him earlier that day with a world record, and given that Liddell had already tired himself in two earlier races that day, Eric's lane position seemed to put the final nail in the coffin on his chances of winning any kind of medal for Scotland.

But Eric was not one to fret. His perspective was quite different from the norm, and his ultimate goal was not to merely win his race or even to compete, but to glorify God. And what the other runners, the crowds, the coaches, and the fans listening to the Games on radios did not know was that Eric had that morning received a reminder of this: as he left his hotel that morning, a British masseur pressed a folded piece of paper into his hand. Liddell thanked the man for it and said he would read the message later.

In his dressing room at the stadium, Liddell unfolded the note and read the following:

It says in the Old Book, "Him that honours me, I will honour." Wishing you the best of success always.[9]

The "Old Book" to which this referred was, of course, the Bible, and the quotation was from 1 Samuel 2:30. Receiving that note deeply touched Eric. As he said a few days later at a dinner in his honor, "It was perhaps the finest thing I experienced in Paris, a great surprise and a great pleasure to know there were others who shared my sentiments about the Lord's day."[10]

Another man who played a role in encouraging Eric that day was fellow Scot Philip Christison, the leader of the Queen's Own Cameron Highlanders. In the moments before Liddell's race began, the regiment's bagpipers played at least part of the rousing "Scotland the Brave." It was a tune and an instrument that would stir the blood of any patriotic Scotsman.

As the runners took their places on the track for the race, Eric, in his typical gentlemanly way, shook the hands of his competitors and wished them well. Moments later, the starting pistol fired, and the men were off. In the stands was Harold Abrahams, who knew something about racing. Abrahams was immediately upset to see that Liddell, unable to see the other runners, had set a blistering pace, as though he were running the 100 meter and not the 400. While pacing was a nonissue in the 100 meter, it was a vital component to the 400 meter. Abrahams could see what Liddell could not, that he had begun too fast and would not be able to keep up the pace.

But Liddell kept it up longer than Abrahams expected. Halfway through the race, he was still ahead by three meters. Although it certainly wasn't possible to continue at this blistering pace, somehow Eric continued.

Back in Edinburgh, seven hundred miles away, Eric's roommate, George Graham-Cumming, listening to the event on a homemade radio, jumped up and shouted the announcer's words as he heard them in his earphones: "They've cleared the last curve. Liddell is still leading! He's increasing his lead! Increasing and increasing! Oh, what a race!"[11]

Increasing? How could that be? But as the runners entered the last hundred meters of the race, that's precisely what took place. And then in the final stretch, Eric went into his odd, familiar end-of-the-race running style, head thrown back, mouth open, arms pounding the air. Moments later, Eric crossed the finish line. He had won the race. Not only did he win, but he beat his nearest competitor by the unfathomable distance of five meters.

Harold Abrahams and anyone else who knew something about the 400 meter were quite agog at what they had witnessed. The stadium crowd exploded with joy, many of them madly waving Union Jacks. Eric Liddell had just won the gold medal for the UK and for Scotland. A few moments later, his time of 47.6 seconds was announced. It was a new world record. Again the crowd exploded.

Sixty years later, in 1984, the American runner Fitch recalled the event: "I had no idea he would win it. Our coach told me not to worry about Liddell because he was a sprinter and he'd pass out 50 yards from the finish."[12] And Fitch's coach should have been correct. After all, that's what logic dictated must happen. Instead, as Fitch recorded in his Olympic diary, "tho a sprinter by practice, [Liddell] ran the pick of the world's quarter milers off their feet."[13]

Few people remember that the 100-meter race was not the only race from which Eric dropped out because it would have required his participation on a Sunday. He also gave up running in the 4 x 100-meter relay and the 4 x 400-meter relay races. When those events were being run on the following Sunday, July 13, Liddell was nowhere near the Olympic stadium. He was in the pulpit at the Scots Kirk in Paris, preaching to a large and admiring audience.

Just two days after his return from Paris and the Olympics, the twenty-two-year-old Eric Liddell graduated with his class from the

University of Edinburgh with a bachelor of science degree. But no one there that day was unaware of the national hero in their midst, and his classmates cheered loudly when Liddell stood to receive his degree. That wasn't all. When that part of the graduation was over, a scrum of his classmates triumphantly and giddily carried Eric on their shoulders all the way to Saint Giles's Cathedral, where the commemoration service was to take place.

Here in the coolness of the great cathedral Liddell once again exhibited his characteristic modesty, humility, and grace. Recalling his visit to the United States for a race the previous year, Liddell said,

> Over the entrance to the University of Pennsylvania, there is written this, "In the dust of defeat as well as in the laurel of victory, there is glory to be found if one has done his best." There are many here who have done their best, but have not succeeded in gaining the laurel of victory. To these, there is as much honour due as to those who have received the laurel of victory.[14]

Following his stunning Olympic victory, Liddell stunned the world again when he announced his plans to stop running altogether. He would become a missionary to China, greatly disappointing all those who hoped to see more of his running. But Eric was excited about the great adventure of it all. He planned to teach science, mathematics, and sports at the Anglo-Chinese College in Tientsin, China. The missionary purpose of the college was to bring the gospel to the sons of wealthy families in the hope of influencing China's future leaders.

In preparation, Eric enrolled in the Scottish Congregational College in Edinburgh for the coming year to study theology. During this year, Eric spent every spare moment accepting the deluge of invitations to speak about his faith during evangelistic campaigns across Scotland. He also taught Sunday school and often preached at his church, Morningside Congregational. As was ever the case and now much more so, Eric's willingness to take part in local sporting competitions as part of evangelistic rallies helped bring out people who would likely never otherwise have attended.

It took the Olympic Games to teach Eric that God intended to use his phenomenal athletic ability to bring people to him. And it was Eric's refusal to run on Sunday, sacrificing an almost certain gold medal, that taught the world there was no hypocrisy in this now world-famous Christian follower. Eric also revealed the value he placed on obedience to God: he ranked it above the greatest treasures the world could offer. His decision to forgo earthly glory brings to mind that scene from the Gospels when Jesus is tempted by Satan in the wilderness:

> The devil took him to a very high mountain and showed him all the kingdoms of the world and their splendor. "All this I will give you," he said, "if you will bow down and worship me." Jesus said to him, "Away from me, Satan! For it is written: 'Worship the Lord your God, and serve him only.'" (Matt. 4:8–10 NIV)

So would Eric Liddell have won the 100-meter race if he had violated his conscience? Recalling the race decades later, Eric's daughter, Patricia, put it this way: "The gold [for the 400 meter] was lovely, but not the most important thing. I truly believe that had he run on Sunday [and] sold out his principles, he would not have won. He would not have had the fire. He was running for God."[15]

Chariots of Fire makes this point as well, when a member of the Olympic Committee explains to another member:

> "The 'lad,' as you call him, is a true man of principles and a true athlete. His speed is a mere extension of his life, its force. We sought to sever his running from himself."
>
> "For his country's sake, yes."
>
> "No sake is worth that. Least of all a guilty national pride."[16]

◆ ◆ ◆

Anyone who watched *Chariots of Fire* may well believe that the most exciting and significant event of Liddell's life was the moment he crossed the finish line in the Olympic 400 meter. One can hardly blame them; after all, that's where the movie ends. We are told that Eric became a missionary to China and that when he died in 1945, all of Scotland mourned.

But the truth—if we can believe it—is that the second half of Eric's life was even more dramatic than the first, although it's not the sort of story one often sees dramatized in major motion pictures. During his years in Scotland, Eric had publicly told thousands of people of his love for God, but in China this love would blossom into service to everyone he encountered.

Eric arrived in China via the Trans-Siberian Railroad in 1925, one year after his Olympic triumph. His parents, his sister, Jenny, and his brother Ernest were all there waiting, delighted to have Eric back with them at last. But the political situation in China was again tense, with feelings running strong against foreigners. This was in part because of a recent deadly clash between colonial police and some demonstrating Chinese.

The Liddells lived in a large house within the compound of the London Missionary Society, in the British concession of Tientsin, and Eric began teaching at the Tientsin Anglo-Chinese College as he had planned. Thanks to his modesty, good humor, and genuine affection for his charges, he quickly became a popular member of the staff. In addition to teaching science classes, he conducted Bible studies, taught Sunday school, coached soccer, and helped with dramatic productions. And of course he spent considerable time improving his Chinese.

Eric also found time to socialize with other missionary families— and one family in particular: the MacKenzies. As it happened, Hugh and Agnes MacKenzie were the parents of a vivacious, red-headed fifteen-year-old daughter, Florence. Over the next few years, Eric, who was ten years Florence's senior, often found excuses to be around her. He saw her during group activities among the missionary families, helped her study, and regularly popped in for tea at her parents' house.

One evening in November 1929, when Florence had turned eighteen, Eric took her for a walk and proposed. Florence—who somehow had no idea Eric was serious about her—excitedly answered yes. Her father agreed to the marriage on the rather draconian condition that Florence first return to Canada and fulfill her goal of becoming a nurse, which meant a three-year separation for the young couple. It would be the first of many long separations throughout their years together.

In 1931, after he completed his initial four-year commitment to work in China, Eric traveled to Canada where he spent four weeks visiting Florence in Toronto. Afterward, he sailed across the Atlantic to Scotland, where he planned to spend his furlough studying at the Scottish Congregational College. By the time he had to return to the mission field, Eric hoped to become an ordained minister.

But while he was in Scotland, others had plans for him too. The London Missionary Society, which was seriously in debt due to the worldwide economic depression, hoped to exploit Eric's tremendous popularity to bring in both money and recruits. Hundreds of churches and athletic groups were also eager to have him speak. The gracious Liddell—who had difficulty saying no—accepted so many speaking engagements during this time that he became exhausted.

Still, despite the endless calls on his time, Eric was ordained on June 22, 1932. After saying good-bye to his family, who were on furlough once more in Scotland, Eric boarded a ship to Canada for another visit with Florence. After a few joyful weeks together, Eric left his fiancée and returned to China, where he once more plunged into the work of the college and the church.

It would be two full years before Florence and her family came to China. They arrived on March 5, 1934, and three weeks later Eric and Florence were at last married. They set up housekeeping in Tientsin, and Florence assisted Eric in his work. She was especially gifted at entertaining students and the children of missionary families in their home, and many of these students made commitments to follow Christ.

Two years after they were married, Eric and Florence had their first child, Patricia Margaret. The next year another daughter, Heather Jean, was born.

By this time, storm clouds were beginning to gather as Japan engaged in acts of aggression against China. In preparation for a possible conflict, the government demanded that the older students at the college undergo military training. As a result, Eric and his colleagues were forced to accommodate changes in the routine of the college. In the summer of 1937, war came to the Chinese in the same way it would come to Americans a few years later: Japanese planes arrived without warning to bomb Tientsin, causing fires, death, and destruction. Within three days the city had fallen to the Japanese.

Chinese refugees, many of them wounded, flooded into the foreign concessions—which were lands in China governed by the British following the Opium Wars. This included Tientsin. Elsewhere in China, the Japanese army committed atrocities on the civilian population, most infamously in Nanking. Still, despite the chaos all around, the Tientsin school opened that September with 575 students.

In dealing with the problems created by the Japanese, Eric sometimes put his life in danger. Once, attempting to relieve a severe coal shortage, he contracted for sixty tons of hard anthracite, but planned to deliver it personally to Siaochang by barge. Two times on the journey armed thieves attacked and robbed him. He was also detained for a day and a half by the Japanese, and then

forced by ragtag military groups to pay exorbitant "taxes." With his money exhausted, he left the barge and journeyed back to Tientsin for a fresh supply of currency. After a mutiny by the crew and a half-day's interrogation by members of the Communist army, he and the coal finally reached Siaochang.[17]

On one memorable occasion, Eric took part in a baptism service as the sound of Japanese artillery shells pounded down and soldiers burst into the building, searching for bandits. On another occasion, Eric rescued a man who had been shot and another who had been nearly decapitated during an attempted execution by the Japanese. On at least one trip, he was himself shot at.

In August 1939, Eric and his wife and daughters were able to escape the difficulties of life in China by traveling to Toronto on furlough for a family visit. After that, they hoped to travel to Great Britain. But, Adolf Hitler altered their plans by invading Poland. Of course this led to war between Great Britain, France, and Germany, and everything changed. To cross the Atlantic, now with German U-boats prowling its waters, was not advisable. So Eric and Florence decided it would be best for Florence to remain in Canada with the girls, while Eric traveled alone to England and Scotland. But Florence and the children so missed him that in March 1940, they boarded a ship, safely crossed the Atlantic, and joined Eric in Scotland. The family spent five happy months there. For a time, despite the ravages of war, they could again enjoy family life.

But their return passage to Canada turned out to be even more dangerous than the previous trip to England. Their ship was part of a fifty-ship convoy, which was accompanied by cargo ships; warships of the Royal Navy provided an escort. Hitler's U-boats found them nonetheless, and a German torpedo struck the ship carrying the Liddells. Happily, it was a dud, and the Liddells survived unharmed. Other ships in their convoy were less fortunate. Before the voyage was finished, the Germans had sunk five of them.

The Liddells visited Canada for a few weeks. Their desire to remain there in a safe place must have been extraordinary, but their desire to obey God's call on their lives as missionaries was stronger still. Even with untold dangers and deprivations ahead, they made the return journey to China, but once there, they were unable to remain together. Florence and the children stayed in Tientsin, but Eric went on to Siaochang, a rural outpost where the London Missionary Society had sent him as a village pastor. Eric regretted that he would no longer be teaching. He was also sorry the dangerous conditions in Siaochang made it impossible to have his family with him.

The first thing Eric noticed when he arrived was how busy the Japanese had been. In a letter to Florence, he wrote: "The last few days we have watched rather depressed and dejected men going out on forced labour, to prepare a motor road to pass to the east of Siaochang." He also wrote his wife, "When I am out it is giving, giving, all the time, and trying to get to know the people, and trying to leave them a message of encouragement and peace in a time when there is no external peace at all."[18]

One day, Liddell conducted a wedding ceremony in a village near Siaochang. During the reception, they could hear the sound of big guns firing.

As he bicycled through the region, Eric often encountered gruesome evidence that the Japanese had visited certain villages. The men had been killed, the women had been raped, homes had been set on fire, and many people were suffering from shock. In the midst of these horrors, Liddell continued to minister to whomever he could, and many came to faith in Christ.

Eric visited his family in Tientsin whenever possible, but as conditions worsened, the Liddells had a hard decision to make. Should Florence and the children stay with Eric in China? Or should they travel to Canada, where they would be safe?

After discussing the problem for months and praying about it, the Liddells decided that the two girls and Florence—now pregnant with their third child—should return to Canada to live with Florence's family. Eric expected to join his family within a year or so. The Liddells traveled to Japan and boarded the Japanese ship on which Florence and the children would travel to Canada. Eric hugged his little girls and asked six-year-old Patricia to help her mother when the new baby came. After kissing his wife good-bye, Eric left the ship. Florence and the children went to the upper deck to search for Eric.

Turning to look back, Eric spotted his family and waved a final good-bye before watching the ship steam away. It would be the last time he saw his family.

Back in Tientsin, where he had been temporarily reassigned, Eric resumed his work. He moved into a flat with his friend A. P. Cullen, whose family had also left China. As the war progressed, garbage collection and other services were disrupted, including mail service. It was not until September that Eric received a cable with the welcome news that his beloved Florence had been safely delivered of their third daughter, Maureen.

After the Japanese forces' craven and infamous attack on Pearl Harbor on December 7, 1941, Liddell's life changed dramatically. At precisely the same time as they were bombing Pearl Harbor, the Japanese were busy in Tientsin, rounding up the foreign military forces responsible for guarding the British, French, and American concessions, installing machine gun emplacements, and making it abundantly clear that they were now in charge. They also sent all the college students home, searched the premises (confiscating a radio), and restricted the movement of all foreigners. They ordered all Americans to move to the British concession, terribly crowding the people who already lived there.

Worst of all for Eric Liddell, the missionaries were no longer allowed to do the work for which they had come to China in the first place. As one biographer notes, "they could no longer teach, preach, or practice medicine. . . . They had become missionaries without a mission."[19]

But Eric was not one to sit idle. He felt that God always had something profitable for him to do. So during these chaotic months he found the time to write a devotional guide that he titled *Discipleship*. Each month had a different theme, such as "The Nature of God," "The Character of Jesus," and "The Holy Spirit." The book is still available today.

One cannot help imagining that his decision not to run on Sunday during the 1924 Olympic Games might have been in his mind as he penned the following words:

> Have you learned to hear God's voice saying, "This is the way, walk ye in it?" Have you learned to obey? Do you realize the tremendous issues that may be at stake?[20]

These words reflected not just that one famous decision but the whole direction of his life. Surely the sacrifice of being alone in a war zone—on the other side of the world from loved ones—was a far greater sacrifice than foregoing the glory of an Olympic medal.

Elsewhere, Liddell wrote,

> If I know something to be true, am I prepared to follow it even though it is contrary to what I want[?] . . . Will I follow if it means being laughed at by friend or foe, or if it means personal financial loss or some kind of hardship?[21]

Eric did his best to help the adults, too, such as willingly rising early to do grocery shopping for them when he could.

In March 1943, the final blow was struck: all foreigners—who were now suddenly considered enemy nationals—were to be sent to an internment camp. After parading them through the streets for a mile as an attempt to humiliate them, the Japanese troops ordered the foreigners onto railway cars.

They were sent to Weihsien, an exhausting journey of some three hundred miles. The three hundred captives—among them missionaries, businessmen, tourists, jazz musicians, prostitutes, and opium addicts—finally arrived at their new home. It was a one-block compound built by Presbyterian missionaries. Its four hundred rooms, hospital, and large church had a few new additions: guard towers, searchlights, and machine guns. Japanese soldiers were now using some of the houses. The Japanese had stripped the buildings of water pipes and had stolen much hospital equipment. As a result of the newly non-existent plumbing, the latrines were unspeakably filthy cesspools. Ironically, the compound was named "Courtyard of the Happy Way."

Nonetheless, the captives quickly set to work tidying up the buildings. In a humble and sacrificial display of true Christian love, Catholic priests and nuns, along with the Protestant missionaries, volunteered to clean out the revolting latrines for the others. The internees built furniture and cooked for each other. High-ranking business executives, accustomed to having everything done for them, learned how to pump water, stoke boiler fires, and peel vegetables.

The internees made time for amusements as well, with musical groups performing everything from sacred music for Easter Sunday, to classical pieces, to jazz. Teachers willingly taught academic courses to anyone who was interested, and when the captives were finished with their daily work, they played card games together.

When the winter of 1943 brought severe cold, the internees made fuel by mixing coal dust with mud in order to keep warm. One priest heroically smuggled food into the camp to complement the children's skimpy diet.

Eric, known as "Uncle Eric" to the children of the camp, lived in tight quarters with his friends Edwin Davis and Joseph McChesney-Clark. As he always had, Eric threw himself heart and soul into his work and volunteer activities. He taught in the camp school; organized softball, basketball, cricket, and tennis games; and planned worship services. He organized square dances and played chess with the kids—anything to keep them out of trouble.

Eric took a special interest in the three hundred children who had been taken out of the China Inland Mission School and were now living in the camp without their parents; he thought of his own three girls, so fortunate to be in better circumstances.

Throughout these difficult years, Liddell maintained his belief that Sundays should be reserved for God. But when teenagers got into a fight during a hockey match, Eric—to the astonishment of those who knew of his famous stand at the 1924 Olympics—agreed to referee the game on the following Sabbath.

Joyce Stranks, who was a seventeen-year-old fellow internee, said that Eric

> came to the feeling that a need existed, [and] it was the Christlike thing to do to let them play with the equipment and to be with them ... because it was more Christlike to do it than to [follow] the letter of the law and let them run amok by themselves. And for me that was very interesting because it was the one thing, of course, everyone remembers about Eric [that he would not run on Sunday because the Sabbath was the Lord's Day].[22]

No matter how busy he was, Eric never neglected his daily time with God. Each morning, Eric and his friend Joe Cotterill woke early and quietly pursued their devotions together by the light of a peanut-oil lamp before beginning a long day of work.

Eric sent monthly Red Cross "letters" to his family, but these messages were limited to an astonishingly terse twenty-five words, and it took many months for these letters to travel back and forth between China and Canada. A year after the internees had been herded into the Courtyard of the Happy Way, Eric wrote a twenty-three-word letter to Florence: "You seem very near today, it is the 10th anniversary of our wedding. Happy loving remembrances, we must celebrate it together next year."[23]

The harsh year had worn down most of the internees, who grew weary of the endless standing in line for everything, from the morning roll call to latrine and shower visits. As the long months wore on, camp residents became less and less concerned about the good of the entire community. Instead, selfishness began to manifest itself. Many began stealing food and other necessities.

Although he deeply missed his family, Eric stayed cheerful for the sake of the others. In a Bible study class, he taught others to love their enemies—including the Japanese guards at their camp—and he exhorted his fellow Christians to pray for them, as the Bible instructed. This one lesson made such an extraordinary impact on Joe Cotterill that he promised God that if he survived the war, he would become a missionary to Japan.

Eric's sincere Christian faith was everywhere on display. Stephen Metcalf, who was seventeen in 1944, remembered one remarkable incident. Metcalf's shoes had completely worn out. One day Eric came to him with something wrapped up in cloth. "Steve," he said, "I see that you have no shoes, and it's winter. Perhaps you can use these." Eric pushed the bundle into Steve's hands. "They were his running shoes," Metcalf says.[24] We can only imagine that Eric had been saving the historic shoes as a memento of his past triumphs, but in the difficult conditions of the internment camp, their practical value to this young man far outweighed their sentimental value to Eric. Others have said that Eric spent much time making peace between various factions of the camp and tried to be a friend to everyone.

◆◆◆

In late 1944, as the internees were about to mark their second full year in the camp, Eric began to experience terrible headaches. Joe Cotterill saw other changes in his friend. He walked and talked more slowly, and his wonderful jokes became a thing of the past. Camp doctors treated him when Eric picked up a flu virus, but the headaches continued nonetheless. Those who knew him best thought he might be suffering from depression, and an old family friend, a Scottish nurse named Annie Buchan, made sure Eric was put back in the hospital where she could keep an eye on him.

Doctors, knowing how hard Eric worked, suggested that he had possibly suffered a nervous breakdown—a diagnosis that deeply disturbed Eric. "I ought to have been able to cast it all on the Lord, and not to have broken down under it," he said bleakly.[25]

On February 11, 1945, Liddell suffered a minor stroke. But just a few days later, he was up and walking around the camp hospital, telling friends he felt much better. The doctors now began to suspect that Eric was suffering from a brain tumor. But without an X-ray machine, they had no way of knowing for sure.

Joyce Stranks visited Eric during breaks from her work in the hospital kitchen, bringing him up to date on what was happening in the camp. On Sunday, February 18, the Salvation Army Band, which played hymns on the Sabbath just outside the hospital, received a special request from Liddell. He wanted them to play "Be Still, My Soul," one of his favorite hymns.

Three days later, Eric typed a letter to his beloved Florence:

Was carrying too much responsibility. Slight nervous breakdown. Am much better after month's rest in hospital. Doctor suggests changing my work. Giving up teaching and athletics and taking on physical work like baking. A good change. So glad to get your letter of July. . . . Special love to yourself and children.[26]

Joyce Stranks dropped in on Eric as he was finishing up the letter. Sitting beside his bed, she and Eric talked about the need to surrender one's will to God in everything one did, "in our attitudes, not what we wanted to do and felt like doing, but what God wanted us to do," Joyce recalled. "He started to say 'surren—surren'—and then his head went back," she said.[27]

The frightened teenager ran to get the nurse, Annie Buchan, but little could be done. Eric had slipped into a coma, and he died that evening at 9:20. He was forty-three.

When news of his death traveled around the camp the next day, the internees were grief-stricken. "He was known, not because of his Olympic prowess," Metcalf recalled, "but because he was Eric. . . . He was the kind of person who was a friend to everyone. And his funeral bore that out. The church wouldn't hold all the people. . . . The whole camp was closed down. It was a very, very moving occasion."[28]

An autopsy revealed that Eric indeed had an inoperable brain tumor. When his death became known to the outside world, many memorial services were held to honor the man who would not run on Sunday—even at the cost of an Olympic gold medal for his country. The news of his death came as a great shock to his wife and daughters in Canada, who thought Eric's strength and vitality would carry him safely through the war.

Many years later, daughter Patricia talked about her thoughts on the day she learned of her father's death, and of how she wondered why God had seen fit to separate Eric from his family during the last four years of his life. "I have met a lot of the children in the camp—the same age as we were," she said,

> and they were put in the camp without their parents. . . . We were safe, and these children did not have their parents, and most of them have done very well. And he made a great influence and steadiness of their lives there. So in that sense, God's hand was there.[29]

Joyce Stranks, who was one of those children to whom Eric was so kind, said, "He made Christ's life so relevant—and made it feel like we who followed Christ must do what He has asked us to do when we are in the situation we are in. You don't get a dispensation because you're in the camp."[30]

Eric's friend A. P. Cullen, who had known Eric most of his life, summed up his friend's life in a camp memorial service on March 3, 1945:

> He was literally God-controlled, in his thoughts, judgements, actions, words to an extent I have never seen surpassed, and rarely seen equalled. Every morning he rose early to pray and read the

Bible in silence: talking and listening to God, pondering the day ahead and often smiling as if at a private joke.[31]

———— ◆ ◆ ◆ ————

At Scotland's Morningside Congregational Church, where Eric had taught, and at Dundas Street Congregational Church in Glasgow, thousands of mourners gathered to honor Eric's life. The *Glasgow Evening News* summed up the feelings of the Scottish people regarding the man who had put God before a gold medal and then served so many others in China: Eric Liddell "did [Scotland] proud every hour of his life."

In 1980, fifty-six years after Eric gave up his chance to win the 100-meter dash, another Scot, Allan Wells, won the 100-meter event at the Moscow Olympics. According to the BBC, "When asked by a journalist if he wanted to dedicate his win to Abrahams, who had died eighteen months previously, Wells replied in typically frank fashion: 'No disrespect to anyone else, but I would prefer to dedicate this to Eric Liddell.'"[32]

And sixty-three years after Eric's death, just before the Beijing Olympic Games, the Chinese government revealed something that even Eric's family didn't know: Eric had been included in a prisoner exchange deal between Japan and Britain but had given up his place to a pregnant woman.

Why does the world still remember and love Eric Liddell today, when other athletes from his era have been long forgotten?

Lord Sands, an Edinburgh civil leader, put his finger on the answer during a dinner honoring Eric just after the 1924 Olympic Games. It was not because Eric was the fastest runner in the world that the guests were gathered there that evening, he said. Instead, "it is because this young man put his whole career as a runner in the balance, and deemed it as small dust, compared to remaining true to his principles."[33]

There are greater issues in life than sport, and the greatest of these is loyalty to the great laws of the soul. Here is a young man who considered the commandment to rest and worship high above the fading laurel crown, and who conquered. It was St. Paul, the tent maker of Tarsus, who watched the Olympic Games many centuries ago and wrote, "They who run in a race run all, but one receiveth the prize. So run that ye may obtain."[34]

God had a far greater plan for Eric Liddell's life than a gold medal that would eventually be forgotten, along with the athlete who won it. And he has great plans for each of us. Those plans may include the need to give up something we value highly. But those who give up what we may most desire—if God has demanded it—the Lord will truly honor.

FOUR

Dietrich Bonhoeffer

1906–45

first heard about Dietrich Bonhoeffer the summer that I turned twenty-five. I was returning to the faith I'd lost at college, and the man who was leading me along that journey gave me a copy of Bonhoeffer's classic book *The Cost of Discipleship*. He asked me if I'd ever heard of Bonhoeffer, and I said that I hadn't. He told me that Bonhoeffer was a German pastor and theologian who, because of his Christian faith, stood up for Germany's Jews and got involved in the plot to assassinate Adolf Hitler. He also said that Bonhoeffer was killed in a concentration camp just three weeks before the end of the war. When I heard all this, I almost couldn't believe it. Was there really a Christian whose faith had led him to heroically stand up against the Nazis at the cost of his own life? It seemed that all the stories I had heard of people taking their faith seriously were negative ones. So this was something new to me, and I instantly wanted to know more about this courageous hero.

One reason I was so interested in Bonhoeffer's story was that I am German. My mother was raised in Germany during the terrible years of Hitler. When she was nine, her father—my grandfather Erich, after whom I'm named—was killed in the war. I always wondered what really happened during that time. How had a great nation of people—of my own people—been drawn down this dark and evil path? My grandmother told me that my grandfather would listen to the BBC with his ear literally pressed against the radio speaker because anyone caught listening to the BBC could be sent to a concentration camp. So I knew that he did not approve of what the Nazis were doing. But he was forced to go to war, like so many men of his generation, and he was killed. My book on Bonhoeffer is dedicated to him.

In many ways, I grew up in the shadow of World War II, and I have always puzzled by the immeasurable evil of the Nazis and the Holocaust. As a result, I've wondered more generally about the question, what is evil and how do we deal with it? The more I know of his life, the more I have come to believe that Bonhoeffer is a powerful role model for us in answering that question.

I remember reading *The Cost of Discipleship* that summer. What Bonhoeffer wrote in that now classic book was every bit as impressive as his amazing life story. His writing had a sparkling clarity and an intensity, and his words bespoke an authentic Christian faith that had no patience for phony religiosity—what Bonhoeffer famously called "cheap grace." As I read that book, I realized that phony religiosity had turned me away from the Christian faith altogether. So it was thrilling to encounter a Christian man who had really lived out his faith, who had put his whole life on the line for what he believed. This was the kind of Christianity that could interest me.

I also learned that this great man of God had somehow felt justified in participating in the plot to assassinate Adolf Hitler. Here was a man who wasn't an armchair theologian, living above the fray. He lived out his faith to the best of his abilities in the real, messy, and often complicated world.

I never intended to write a biography about anyone, much less Dietrich Bonhoeffer. I always say that I'm far too self-centered to want to spend several years thinking about someone else. Nonetheless, I wrote *Amazing Grace*, the biography of William Wilberforce, which came out in 2007, and after that book, people kept asking me, "Who are you going to write about next?" I didn't want to write another biography, but people kept asking the question. Eventually I thought that I might write one more. And there was just one person besides the great William Wilberforce who had captivated my heart and soul and mind such that I would be willing to devote a whole book to him. Needless to say, that man was Dietrich Bonhoeffer. My biography of him came out on the sixty-fifth anniversary of his death.

For a number of reasons, the book struck a chord with many and became a best seller. It has revived interest in Bonhoeffer and his work in a way that I never could have dreamed and that I find deeply gratifying. As a result of writing the book, I've had the honor of meeting two US presidents, and everywhere I go, the message of Bonhoeffer seems to get people talking and debating and thinking. And acting. That's the best part. It's an amazing and profound story that continues to touch and change people's lives, and I'm thrilled to be able to share a short version of it here.

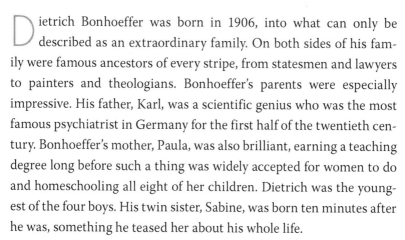

Dietrich Bonhoeffer was born in 1906, into what can only be described as an extraordinary family. On both sides of his family were famous ancestors of every stripe, from statesmen and lawyers to painters and theologians. Bonhoeffer's parents were especially impressive. His father, Karl, was a scientific genius who was the most famous psychiatrist in Germany for the first half of the twentieth century. Bonhoeffer's mother, Paula, was also brilliant, earning a teaching degree long before such a thing was widely accepted for women to do and homeschooling all eight of her children. Dietrich was the youngest of the four boys. His twin sister, Sabine, was born ten minutes after he was, something he teased her about his whole life.

All eight children were as remarkable as their parents. Dietrich's eldest brother, Karl Friedrich, went into physics, and at age twenty-three he was involved in splitting the atom with Max Planck and Albert Einstein. Bonhoeffer's middle brother, Klaus, became the head of the legal department at Lufthansa. His sisters were brilliant and married brilliant men. But the way in which they all used their great minds is what made them particularly impressive.

Karl Bonhoeffer taught his children that having a remarkable IQ was of no use if one didn't train one's mind to think clearly and logically. As a scientist, he believed that was of paramount importance. One must learn to follow the evidence and the facts and the logic all the way through to the end. Sloppy thinking of any kind was not tolerated in the Bonhoeffer household. One would surely think twice before opening one's mouth at the dinner table because all statements would immediately be challenged. This early training in how to think was at the core of the Bonhoeffer children's upbringing, and it was one reason that Dietrich grew up to have the tremendous impact on those around him that he did.

Perhaps even more important in the Bonhoeffer family was acting upon what one said one believed. One must not only think clearly but must prove one's thoughts *in action*. If one was unprepared to live out what one claimed to believe, perhaps one didn't believe what one claimed after all! So it was from an early age that Dietrich understood that ideas were never mere ideas but the foundations upon which one built one's actions and ultimately one's life. Ideas and beliefs must be tried and tested because one's life might depend on them. This would hold true in the worlds of science and theology alike.

The Bonhoeffer family was also culturally sophisticated. All of them read great literature and memorized great poems and traveled widely. They were devoted to music, attending operas and concerts whenever possible. Dietrich was a bit of a musical virtuoso. He could play several instruments, was able to sight-read, and was composing and arranging music at an early age. Each Saturday the Bonhoeffer family had a musical evening where they gathered to play instruments or sing. This family tradition continued for many years.

In other ways, Dietrich was a typical boy, sometimes getting into fights in school and needing to be disciplined, but more typically expressing his boyish energies in more positive ways. Later in life, Bonhoeffer loved taking part in athletics; the only movie we have of Bonhoeffer—although it is just a few seconds long—is a home movie of him tossing a ball. You can see this clip in the excellent Bonhoeffer documentary directed by my friend Martin Doblmeier.

As with most Germans of that era, Dietrich was raised in the Lutheran Church. His family members were not big churchgoers, but there was a Christian atmosphere in the home, mainly due to Bonhoeffer's mother. She read the children Bible stories, and the governesses she hired were devout Christians. Bonhoeffer's father seems to have been an agnostic, but he deeply respected his wife's faith. He graciously supported her efforts to raise the children as Christians and always participated in family gatherings where Scriptures were read and hymns were sung.

◆ ◆ ◆

When Dietrich was eight, World War I arrived. Before it ended in 1918, all three of his older brothers were old enough to enlist and proudly did so. The Bonhoeffers were not chest-beating German nationalists, but they had a healthy sense of patriotism and were glad to take part in defending their country, as they saw it. In 1917, Dietrich's brother Walter, the youngest of his three brothers, was called to the front. The whole family saw him off at the station, and his mother ran alongside the train carriage as it pulled away, saying, "It is only space that separates us."[1] Two weeks later the unthinkable happened: Walter was killed. His death was utterly devastating to the family, and Dietrich's mother had what seems to have been a nervous breakdown. For some months she lived with the neighbors, and it was years before she was herself again. Dietrich was deeply affected by it.

About a year later, when Dietrich was thirteen, he made the fateful decision to pursue a career in theology. Not many thirteen-year-olds know what they want to do when they grow up, and those who do rarely decide to become theologians! But the Bonhoeffers took academics very seriously, and the idea of a life in the world of academics seemed perfectly normal. But only up to a point: of all the academic disciplines Dietrich might have chosen, theology was one about which his father had serious reservations. His older brothers were similarly mystified by the choice. So they and Dietrich's older sisters and their friends teased him about it. Yet he was not to be dissuaded. He had thought it through quite thoroughly and met his siblings' needling skepticism with firm resolve.

In his choice of theology, Dietrich was following in the footsteps of his mother's side of the family. Indeed, Dietrich's maternal grandfather was a theologian, as was his maternal great-grandfather, who was quite famous. When Dietrich was a student, his great-grandfather's theological textbooks were still being used, and a statue of him stands today in Jena. So Bonhoeffer's mother likely approved of her youngest son's ambitions.

That same year Dietrich took a confirmation class at the local Lutheran church. At the end of the class, the pastor gave Scripture verses to everyone. Many years later, an old woman who had been in that class with Dietrich Bonhoeffer said she had received the same Scripture verse as Dietrich. It read: "Blessed is the man who remains steadfast under trial, for when he has stood the test, he will receive the crown of life, which God has promised to those who love him."[2]

When he turned seventeen in 1923, Dietrich enrolled at Tübingen University to begin his theological studies. The medieval city of Tübingen is located on the Neckar River, and during his semester there, Bonhoeffer sometimes went skating. One day he slipped and struck his head so hard that he lay unconscious for some time. When his father learned of the accident, he and his wife sped to Tübingen to be with their boy. As a psychiatrist, Karl Bonhoeffer knew a long period of unconsciousness could mean trouble, and after the death of their beloved Walter a few years earlier, the Bonhoeffer parents were understandably anxious to be as close to their children as possible whenever there was any danger or crisis. So they immediately got on a train from Berlin to make sure that everything possible was being done for their son.

To everyone's relief, Dietrich recovered quickly. And as it happened, his parents' unplanned visit coincided with his eighteenth birthday. So what began as an unpleasant emergency ended as a happy celebration. It was during this time that Dietrich had the idea of taking a trip to Rome. He had studied so much about Rome over the years and traveled there in his mind so often that when the idea of actually going there came up, he was giddy with anticipation. His parents weren't thrilled about the idea, but eventually they were willing for him to go if his older brother Klaus accompanied him, and that spring, they went.

Dietrich knew it would probably be extremely enjoyable and educational, but he didn't know that it would be so significant to his future. It was in Rome that, for the first time, Dietrich thought seriously about the question that would dominate his thinking for the rest of his life. That question was: What is the church?

It first came into his mind with real power on Palm Sunday when he was visiting Saint Peter's Basilica. Although not himself a Roman Catholic, Bonhoeffer had great respect for the Catholic Church and attended many Catholic services during his Roman holiday. But that Palm Sunday he saw for the first time in his life people of every race and color celebrating the Eucharist together. This picture struck him with the force of an epiphany. He suddenly saw the church as something universal and eternal, as something that transcended race and nationality and culture, as something that went far beyond Germany and far beyond Lutheranism. He made the intellectual connection that would affect everything going forward: all who called on the name of Jesus Christ were his brothers and sisters, even if they were nothing like him in any other way. This idea would have far-reaching consequences, especially once the Nazis took power. But that would not be for some time.

When Bonhoeffer returned from Rome, he did not go back to Tübingen. Instead he enrolled at Berlin University, which was the most prestigious institution in the world for theological studies in the 1920s. The legendary Friedrich Schleiermacher had taught there in the latter part of the nineteenth century, and the living legend Adolf von Harnack was still teaching there. Bonhoeffer studied with him and knew him very well. They often commuted to the university together on the trolley. Bonhoeffer was not a theological liberal like Harnack, but he respected him and the other theological liberals at Berlin University and learned much from them. Throughout his life, Bonhoeffer was not afraid to learn from those with whom he disagreed.

Bonhoeffer earned his PhD at the startlingly young age of twenty-one. In his postgraduate work, the question he was asking and answering on a high theological and academic level was the same one that had entered his head on that Palm Sunday in Rome: What is the church?

In the course of answering that question, Bonhoeffer discovered that he actually wanted to work in the church as well. He wanted not only to be an academic theologian but also to become an ordained Lutheran minister. But in Germany in those days, one couldn't be ordained until one was twenty-five. So, at age twenty-two, he traveled to Barcelona and served there for a year as an assistant vicar in a German-speaking congregation. Then at age twenty-four, with another year before he could be ordained, he decided to study at Union Theological Seminary in the United States.

◆ ◆ ◆

Since he had earned a PhD in theology from the prestigious Berlin University three years earlier, it can be assumed Bonhoeffer was not principally going to New York for the academic experience. It seems that he was mostly interested in the culturally broadening aspect of a year in America. But what happened to Bonhoeffer during his nine-month sojourn in New York ended up being much more than a culturally broadening experience.

It all began when Bonhoeffer befriended a fellow student named Frank Fisher, an African American from Alabama. The social work component of Fisher's Union studies involved spending time at Abyssinian Baptist Church in Harlem. So one Sunday in the autumn of 1930, Fisher invited Bonhoeffer to join him there. Bonhoeffer was only too eager to go along.

Abyssinian Baptist Church was then the largest church in the United States, and what Bonhoeffer saw there that Sunday staggered him. The vast congregation of African Americans wasn't merely "doing church" or going through the motions; on the contrary, the people in attendance that morning seemed to take their faith very seriously. For most of these people, life was hard, and the God they worshipped was real and personal. He was not a philosophical or theological construct. Bonhoeffer witnessed something that morning more palpable and visceral than anything he had seen in a church before. The worship was more than hymn singing; it was powerful and real; and the preaching was too. The fiery pastor, Adam Clayton Powell Sr., exhorted his hearers not just to have a genuine relationship with Jesus but also to translate that into action in their lives, to care for the poor and do the other things that Jesus urged his followers to do.

The patrician twenty-four-year-old was so moved that morning that he decided to go up to Harlem every Sunday afterward. It was extremely unusual for a blond, bespectacled Berlin academic to be involved in a black church in Harlem, but Bonhoeffer was there often in the months ahead. He even taught a Sunday school class. He became very involved in the lives of the congregation and in the budding issue of civil rights. For perhaps the first time in his life, Bonhoeffer seemed to link the idea of having deep faith in Jesus with taking political and social action. He always knew that real faith in Jesus must lead to action, not just to philosophical and theological thinking; it had to manifest itself in one's life. But the profound faith of the African

Americans in New York, and their struggle for equality, helped him see this in a new way.

Of course Bonhoeffer made the connection to the oppression of the Jews when he returned to Germany, but we don't know whether he made this connection while he was still in New York. On the surface, the Jews of Germany—unlike the African Americans in New York—had enjoyed notable economic and cultural success. It was impossible at that time to imagine the horrors that lay ahead for them. After all, Hitler would not be elected chancellor and president of Germany for several years.

One episode in New York perhaps shows that God knew Bonhoeffer would have an important role in helping Germany's Jews in the years to come. On Easter Day in 1931—the only Easter that Bonhoeffer spent in America—he couldn't get into any of the big mainline Protestant churches. He very much wanted to experience an Easter service in one of them, but he discovered too late that since everyone goes to church on Easter, no seats were available. One literally needed to get a ticket well in advance of the day. So, what did Dietrich do? He went to a synagogue to hear Rabbi Stephen Wise preach. In truth, it wasn't an actual synagogue; it was Carnegie Hall. Rabbi Wise had such a large following that his services couldn't be contained in any of the existing New York synagogues.

The events of the nine months Bonhoeffer spent in America had a profound effect on him, and when he returned to Germany in the summer of 1931, it was clear to his friends that something had changed. He seemed to take his faith much more seriously. Before he had left, his intellect had been in the right place, but somehow now his heart was engaged in a way that it hadn't been before.

Bonhoeffer took a position on the theological faculty of Berlin University and began to teach there. From behind the lectern, he would say things that one did not usually hear in Berlin theological circles.

For example, he referred to the Bible as the *Word of God*, as though God existed and was alive and wanted to speak to us through it. The whole point of studying the text was to get to the God *behind* the text. The experience could not be merely intellectual but must also be personal and real, as it had been for the African American Christians at Abyssinian Baptist Church in New York City. Bonhoeffer also took his students on retreats and taught them how to pray. One of his students said that Bonhoeffer once asked him: "Do you love Jesus?"

Bonhoeffer had changed, but Germany had changed too. Before Bonhoeffer left for New York in 1930, the Nazis had very little political power. They were then the ninth most important political party in the Reichstag, the German parliament. But when he returned in 1931, they had vaulted to being the second most important party and were consolidating more power with each day that passed. Bonhoeffer could see the trouble on the horizon, and he would speak in his classes about it. He was not afraid of saying things like, "For German Christians, there can be only one savior, and that savior is Jesus Christ."[3] That was a brave statement because many Germans were beginning to look toward Hitler as their savior, as the man who would lead them out of the wilderness and suffering of the previous several years.

And who could have guessed what lay ahead under his leadership? Hitler presented himself as a man of moderation and peace, as someone devoted to the German people, and as someone who publicly claimed to be following "God's will." He promised to lead Germany out of the economic hell into which it had fallen, and to lift the deep shame that Germans felt at having lost the First World War.

Hitler fed the idea that they had lost the war because they had been betrayed from within, by Communists and Jews—he often conflated these terms—and he said that the way forward was to purge Germany of these supposed traitors. This idea of treachery from within Germany was known as the *Dolchstoss* (stab-in-the-back) legend, and many accepted it as the main reason that Germany had lost the war.

Hitler also portrayed himself as the one who might lead Germans beyond the humiliation of the Versailles Treaty, through which the victorious Allied powers had imposed unbearable terms on the Germans. The Germans bore deep resentment toward the other European powers, especially France. Hitler brilliantly played upon these various factors. As a result, the average German was only too willing to take a chance on him. After all, what could be worse than what Germany had been enduring?

But Bonhoeffer saw that things could get much worse and likely would. He had an innate sense that the National Socialists would lead Germans into far darker places than they had yet been, and he was one of the very few voices who spoke out against it.

◆ ◆ ◆

Bonhoeffer's first opportunity to speak out on a large stage came shortly after Hitler became chancellor in late January 1933. Just two days later, Bonhoeffer gave a famous speech on the radio in which he dissected the so-called "Führer Principle." This was one of the many half-baked philosophical ideas that had aided Hitler's rise to power.

Führer is the German word for "leader," and the Führer Principle was the idea that Germany needed a strong leader to lead it out of the morass of the Weimar Republic. It all seemed perfectly logical. After all, before their loss in the First World War, Germans had strong leadership under the kaiser, and after they lost the war and the Allies insisted that the kaiser abdicate the throne, everything went sour.

The Allies had imposed a democratic government on Germany, but without a tradition of democracy the Germans simply didn't know how to govern themselves. The Weimar government seemed rudderless, and the results were horrific. There were long bread lines and rampant unemployment and vicious political squabbles. Surely things had been better under the strong leadership of the kaiser! And surely any strong leader would be better than what they now had! The Nazis exploited this idea brilliantly, presenting Hitler as the one-man solution to all of Germany's ills. He would be a strong leader! He would lead Germany back to her glory days under the kaiser!

The only problem was that Hitler's idea of leadership had nothing to do with authentic leadership, and Bonhoeffer made this crystal clear in his radio speech. Bonhoeffer explained that true authority must, by definition, be submitted to a higher authority—which is to say, God—and true leadership must be servant leadership. This notion was precisely the opposite of the idea embodied in the Führer Principle and in Hitler. So, just two days after Hitler became Germany's chancellor, Bonhoeffer was publicly on the record against him and his perverse idea of leadership. Bonhoeffer explained that the idol worship that Hitler was encouraging would make him not a leader but a "misleader." He would mislead the German people, with tragic results.

Somehow Bonhoeffer saw from the very beginning what no one else seemed to see—that Hitler and the philosophy he represented would end tragically, and that Nazi ideology could not coexist with Christianity.

Most Germans had no idea that Hitler in fact despised Christianity. He thought it a weak religion, and he desperately wished that Germany could be rid of it as soon as possible. Of course he could never say this publicly, since most Germans thought of themselves as good Lutheran Christians. So Hitler pretended to be a Christian because he knew that saying what he really believed would erode his political power.

Hitler's goal was to slowly infiltrate the church with Nazi ideology and to take it over from the inside. He wanted to unify all the German churches and create a single state church that submitted to him alone. But he would do it a step at a time to avoid drawing attention to his efforts. And like the proverbial frog in the pot of boiling water, the German people would not realize what was happening until it was too late.

Bonhoeffer tried to warn his fellow Christians of Hitler's intentions. Not only did he have a brilliant mind that had been trained well by his scientist father to think logically and see things through to the end, but Bonhoeffer also seemed to have an uncanny sense of what was happening in Germany. His personal relationship with God and his deep study of the Scriptures helped him see what his mere intellect could not, so he was one of the leading and prophetic voices for the church in his time.

Bonhoeffer knew that true Christians in Germany had to stand against the Nazified state "church" of Adolf Hitler. They had to fight with everything they had while there was still a chance to fight. He devoted a large part of his life trying to wake up the church to what was happening. A slumbering church would be no match for the Nazis, and Bonhoeffer did all he could to get others to recognize that they must prevent the Nazis from imposing their ideology on all German Christians.

The main issue in the battle was the Nazi idea that all things must be seen through a racial lens. According to the Nazis, Germans must be "racially" pure, so they tried to purge the German church of all "Jewish elements." Bonhoeffer regarded this as an absurdity. Jesus was a Jew, as were almost all the early Christians, and Christianity is at its core fundamentally Jewish. To excise all "Jewish elements" from it would destroy the very essence of the Christian faith. Of course that was precisely the Nazis' goal.

One of Bonhoeffer's closest friends, Franz von Hildebrand, was ethnically Jewish, but his family had converted to Christianity and he had been ordained as a Lutheran minister. According to the Nazi idea of what should constitute the German church, all ethnically Jewish men must leave the "German" church. Bonhoeffer knew that the God of Scripture looks on the heart of a person, not at his ethnic background. In the end, a frustrated Bonhoeffer led the way for a number of pastors to leave the increasingly Nazified official German church, and they formed what became known as the Confessing Church.

Bonhoeffer was perhaps the first of his countrymen to see that Christians were obliged to speak out for those who could not, to "be a voice for the voiceless." In the case of Nazi Germany, that meant the Jews. At one point Bonhoeffer made the incendiary statement that "only he who stands up for the Jews may sing Gregorian chants."[4] What he meant was that if we were not heroically and courageously doing what God wanted us to do, God was not interested in our public displays of worship. To sing to God when we were not doing what God called us to do was to be a hypocrite. Many were offended at Bonhoeffer's outspokenness on these issues. But he insisted that Jesus was the "man for others,"[5] and to follow Jesus meant to stand up for the dignity of those others who were different from us.

In some ways the formation of the Confessing Church was a victory for all serious Christians in Germany. But Bonhoeffer was not as encouraged as others were. He seemed to sense that despite the victories they had along the way, it would not end well. He felt that most Christians in Germany—including those within the Confessing Church—did not acknowledge what was really at stake and were unwilling to fight the Nazis with everything they had. They seemed to think that whatever problems existed could be fixed eventually. But Bonhoeffer knew that if the Christians in Germany did not wake up to the radical evil growing in their midst and do all they could to eradicate it, all would soon be lost.

Martin Niemöller, who was Bonhoeffer's friend and colleague in the Confessing Church leadership, was someone who saw what was happening, but when he finally saw it, it was too late. He wrote a famous statement about this:

> First they came for the socialists, and I did not speak out—
>   because I was not a socialist.
> Then they came for the trade unionists, and I did not speak out—
>   because I was not a trade unionist.
> Then they came for the Jews, and I did not speak out—
>   because I was not a Jew.
> Then they came for me—and there was no one left to speak for me.[6]

◆ ◆ ◆

n 1935, Bonhoeffer was called upon to lead an illegal seminary in the Confessing Church. There at Finkenwalde he would train

seminarians not to be merely Lutheran clerics but true and obedient disciples of Jesus Christ. The years he spent doing this may
be thought of as the Golden Age of Bonhoeffer. He wrote about
this time in his classic book *Life Together*, telling what it means to
live in a Christian community, one that takes the Sermon on the
Mount very seriously. He taught the seminarians how to maintain a
robust devotional life, praying and studying and meditating on the
Scriptures daily.

Some of the more traditional Lutheran leaders were disturbed by
what they heard about Bonhoeffer's experiment in living in a community of faith at Finkenwalde. But Bonhoeffer felt that to fight evil, one
must train Christians how to pray, how to worship God, and how to
actually behave as though these things were true. It was not just about
theory and theology. It was about real life. Bonhoeffer was a maverick
in that sense. He was helping the young seminarians learn how to live
out their faith.

Eventually, the Gestapo shut down Finkenwalde. After all, it was
an illegal seminary that had taken a public stand against the policies
of the Third Reich. Yet Bonhoeffer continued to teach the young men.
He would just have to do it in a clever way, shielded from the prying
eyes of the Gestapo. For several years he managed to continue teaching underground. The students lived with pastors in the area and
gathered in ways that didn't attract the attention of outsiders. The
Gestapo didn't know where the training was happening—sometimes
it was in a farmhouse here, and at other times it was in a pastor's
vicarage there—so they were unable to stop it for quite some time.
But as the Nazis were nothing if not meticulous and relentless, they
did stop it eventually.

By the late 1930s, Bonhoeffer's possibilities for openly serving
God in Germany were being winnowed down to nothing. The Nazis
kept increasing the scope of government with more and more laws
and regulations, constricting and choking off the liberties of every
German and especially of serious Christians. As the noose tightened,

there was less and less that Bonhoeffer could do. After the Nazis forbade him from teaching, they prevented him from speaking publicly. Finally they prevented him from publishing because he had the temerity to write a book on the Psalms. The Nazi ideologues who had tried to purge the German church of all Jewish elements thought that the Psalms and everything in the Old Testament were too Jewish and must be avoided altogether. It may sound absurd and even comical that they would consider such a thing, but for the German Christians at the time it was all deadly serious.

In 1938 and 1939, war clouds were on the horizon. Bonhoeffer knew that when hostilities were declared, his conscience would not allow him to pick up a gun and fight in Hitler's war. Bonhoeffer wasn't a pacifist in our contemporary understanding of that term, but the war that Hitler was bringing to Europe and the world was not a just war in the Christian sense. It was not a war of last resort but a war of pure nationalist aggression. So he prayed earnestly, asking God to show him what to do. It was impossible to declare oneself a conscientious objector in the Third Reich. Nor did he want to take a public stand against fighting in the war, because as a leading figure in the Confessing Church, he could get everyone else in the Confessing Church in trouble. How could he avoid having to fight while not endangering his brethren in the Confessing Church?

Bonhoeffer found a way out: he would go to America, perhaps to teach at Union or elsewhere. If an invitation were proffered and he went to the United States before the outbreak of war, it would be impossible for him to return to Germany. He would be obliged to ride things out across the Atlantic until the war was over. The famous American theologian Reinhold Niebuhr got involved, pulling some strings and wangling an invitation for Bonhoeffer to come back to Union Theological Seminary, where Niebuhr was then teaching. Everything was arranged, and in early June 1939 Dietrich Bonhoeffer once more sailed for America.

But no sooner was he on board the ship than Bonhoeffer began to feel uneasy about his decision. Had he missed God's will? He prayed earnestly, asking God to lead him, to show him what to do. In my book about him I quote at length from Bonhoeffer's copious diary entries and letters during this period. It's a privilege to have this window into his private thoughts as he wrestled with his future at this crucial time. Bonhoeffer obviously expected the Author of the Scriptures to speak to him through those Scriptures, and each day he meditated on the verse of the day, trusting God to guide him.

When Bonhoeffer arrived in New York, the uneasiness did not lift. Indeed, it intensified. He felt terribly lonely and out of place. What was he doing in America when his people were about to undergo such a terrible ordeal? In the end he really believed that God wanted him to go back, to stand with his people, come what may. He knew that danger and possibly death lay ahead, but he went nonetheless.

Bonhoeffer left New York in early July, only twenty-six days after his arrival. The ship steamed out of New York Harbor at midnight, under a full moon. When he arrived in Germany, his friends were shocked to see him. "What are you doing here?" they demanded. "We have arranged things at great difficulty so that you could escape, so that you be spared and be of use to Germany after all of this trouble blows over. Why did you return?" Bonhoeffer was not one to mince words. "I made a mistake," he said.[7] Nonetheless, it didn't answer the pressing question of what exactly he *would* be doing in Germany now.

To understand what he would do, we need to understand that Bonhoeffer's family had been involved in the conspiracy against Hitler for years. They were already having secret conversations about what to do about Hitler in early 1933, just after Hitler had become chancellor. These conversations had continued throughout the decade as Hitler consolidated his power. The Bonhoeffers were exceedingly well connected in elite Berlin circles, and they were also close to a number of the key players in what would emerge as a widespread conspiracy against Hitler. During these years, Dietrich was involved in these conversations, often providing moral support to the conspirators and giving them solid theological reasons to fuel their involvement in their dangerous conspiracy against the German head of state.

Most Germans would not have been comfortable taking any stand or action against their nation's leader. But Bonhoeffer thought the matter through on a much deeper level than most Germans. He believed that to do anything less was to shrink from God's call to act upon one's beliefs. And this included standing up for those who were being persecuted, come what may. To do anything less would be to buy into the idea of "cheap grace" that he had so eloquently written about.

But now that Bonhoeffer had returned and war had broken out, what exactly *would* he do? The time for merely providing moral support to others had passed. For Bonhoeffer, now was the time to get actively involved. But how?

The member of Bonhoeffer's family who was most directly involved in the conspiracy was his sister Christel's husband, Hans von Dohnanyi. Dohnanyi was a leading figure in German military intelligence, called the Abwehr, and the Abwehr was at the very center of the conspiracy against Hitler. His brother-in-law hired Dietrich to work for the Abwehr, ostensibly to use his talents to help the Third Reich during this time of war. But the reality of his role couldn't have been more different. Bonhoeffer had officially joined the conspiracy, and he essentially now had become a double agent.

As an Abwehr agent, Bonhoeffer was able to travel outside Germany to neutral countries such as Sweden and Switzerland. But the real reason he went was to secretly get word to the Allies that there were Germans inside Germany who were working against Adolf Hitler. Bonhoeffer's best friend, Eberhard Bethge, said it was at this point that Bonhoeffer went from "confession to conspiracy."[8] He was openly pretending to be a part of the Third Reich, but in reality he was secretly working to destroy it.

Although he had been officially prohibited from publishing,

Bonhoeffer continued to write. He now worked on his magnum opus, *Ethics.* He never completely finished the work, but Bethge had it published after Bonhoeffer's death.

I n 1942, Bonhoeffer was visiting one of his dearest friends and supporters, Ruth von Kleist-Retzow, at her home in Pomerania, when he noticed her eighteen-year-old granddaughter, Maria. Bonhoeffer had known Maria since she was twelve, but because he was eighteen years older than she was, he had always regarded her as a child. A chance meeting that day changed that idea. For many reasons it was an extremely unlikely pairing. But the times were tumultuous for everyone. Maria lost her father and her dearest brother in the war during this year, and she turned toward Bonhoeffer for pastoral comfort. Over the weeks and months the relationship bloomed into something else, and in the spring of 1943, they were engaged.

Although Maria's mother was not pleased with the situation, she eventually came around to accepting it. But no sooner had she agreed to let Dietrich and Maria make their engagement public than Bonhoeffer was arrested. The arrest took place at his parents' home in the Charlottenburg neighborhood of Berlin in April. Bonhoeffer was not then arrested for his role in the plot to kill Hitler because that plot and the wider conspiracy against the Nazi leader had not yet been uncovered. He was arrested for something much less serious, comparatively speaking—for his involvement in a plan to save the lives of seven German Jews.

Leaders of the Gestapo had been suspicious of fishy activity in the Abwehr for some time. For months they kept their eyes on Bonhoeffer, Dohnanyi, and a few others. They had even tapped their telephones. When they discovered a secret plan to get these Jews (the number had grown from seven to fourteen) out of Germany and into neutral Switzerland, the Gestapo had enough information to make an arrest.

Bonhoeffer was taken to Tegel military prison in Berlin, just seven miles from his home. This was not nearly as bad as if he had been taken to the underground Gestapo prison. Bonhoeffer's uncle was the military commandant over Berlin, so while at Tegel, Bonhoeffer was treated reasonably well. It was at Tegel that he wrote most of his now famous *Letters and Papers from Prison* and a number of poems, including his most famous poem, "Who Am I?" Bonhoeffer was by all accounts a picture of peace and quiet joy during his days in prison. Many of his fellow prisoners and even some of the guards later related that he had been a profound comfort to them amidst the uncertainty and dangers of that time.

Bonhoeffer was hopeful that he would eventually be released. He believed that he could probably outfox the prosecutor and prove his innocence when his case came to trial. That was his firm hope, as well as the hope of his fiancée and his family. But Bonhoeffer had two other scenarios in mind that would lead to his release: first, even if his case didn't come to trial, or if it came to trial and he lost, he thought that the Allies might win the war and the Nazis would be removed from power. And second and closer to home, he hoped that the conspirators who hadn't yet been arrested would succeed in killing Hitler and his top lieutenants. That way the whole nightmare would be over. Of course things did not end so well.

What happened instead, fifteen months after his arrest—on July 20, 1944—was that the famous Valkyrie plot went into action. And failed. There were earlier failed attempts to kill Hitler, but in those cases, the bombs had somehow never exploded. The Valkyrie plot was the first time that a bomb actually exploded, yet it failed to kill Hitler. But precisely because it had exploded, the vast conspiracy to assassinate Hitler was for the first time exposed.

Upon learning of the conspiracy, Hitler was beside himself with rage. It put him in mind of the *Dolchstoss* legend from the First World War, which claimed that Germany had been destroyed by traitors within its ranks. This thought was too much for the thin-skinned dictator to bear, so he ordered the arrest and torture of thousands. Names were revealed, and one of those names was Dietrich Bonhoeffer. He was suddenly known to be not just a pastor and academic who had theological difficulties with the Nazi regime; he was now known to be a leader in the conspiracy to kill Adolf Hitler.

At this point, Bonhoeffer knew that his days were probably numbered. In October 1944, he was transferred to the Gestapo's underground high-security prison, where he was threatened with torture. It doesn't seem that he was tortured, but his brother Klaus and brother-in-law Dohnanyi.

This was now the end of 1944, and the war was winding down. Hitler—increasingly unmoored from reality—believed that history had a grand and noble victory in store for him. But most Germans understood that they were not winning and could not win.

In February 1945, endless squadrons of Allied planes bombed Berlin with such intensity that the Germans decided to transfer all prisoners held at the Gestapo prison to other locations. Bonhoeffer was transferred to the Buchenwald concentration camp where he remained for two months. Then, as April dawned, he was taken on a week-long journey that eventually would take him to Flossenbürg concentration camp, and there, on the direct orders of Hitler, early on the morning of April 9, 1945, he was executed by hanging.

◆ ◆ ◆

Most people, on hearing of Bonhoeffer's death, regard it as a sad and tragic ending. And of course to some great extent it is precisely that. The idea that this profoundly good and brilliant thirty-nine-year-old man who was engaged to a beautiful young woman was executed just three weeks before the end of the war is nothing if not tragic and sad. But if we stop there, we miss the larger and more important reality. We miss precisely what Bonhoeffer lived his whole life to illustrate and what he most desperately wanted each of us to realize: that anyone who pays a price or who suffers for obeying God's will is worthy of our celebration, not our pity. And if someone goes to his death as a result of obeying God's will, this is even more true.

Bonhoeffer's beliefs about the subject of death in general help us understand how he viewed his own death. We hardly need to speculate, though, since he wrote and delivered a sermon on death in 1933. In that sermon he said, "No one has yet believed in God and the Kingdom of God, no one has yet heard about the realm of the resurrected, and not been homesick from that hour—waiting and looking forward to being released from bodily existence." He continued,

> How do we know that dying is so dreadful? Who knows whether in our human fear and anguish, we are only shivering and shuddering at the most glorious, heavenly blessed event in the world? Death is hell and night and cold, if it is not transformed by our faith. But that is just what is so marvelous, that we can transform death.[9]

In a poem written in the last year of his life, likely knowing that death lay ahead for him, Bonhoeffer called death "the last station on the road to freedom."[10] As a devout Christian, Bonhoeffer worshipped a God who had emphatically conquered death in Jesus Christ through the Crucifixion and the resurrection. Understanding this historical and theological fact—and its far-reaching implications—is unavoidably at the core of the Christian faith, and he went to great lengths to communicate this.

In his 1933 sermon, Bonhoeffer exhorted his hearers to consider this idea, and in the poem he wrote in 1944 he did so again. For him the knowledge that the God of Scripture had actually come to earth and had conquered death changed everything. It gave Bonhoeffer the courage to do all that he did in life, and it gave him the courage to face his own death without fear and trembling. By all accounts, Bonhoeffer faced danger and the gallows with deep peace. What he wrote and said and how he lived and died encourage and inspire us to face our own lives and the evil around us, including the specter of death, with that same deep faith and fearlessness.

◆ ◆ ◆

On the day that Bonhoeffer was executed, the crematorium at Flossenbürg was broken. So Bonhoeffer shared the fate of the innumerable Jews who had recently been killed just as he had been: his body was tossed on a pile and burned. But it seems clear that, for Bonhoeffer, giving his life for the Jews was an honor. The God of the Jews had called him to give his life for the Jews. So it would also have been an honor to have his body disposed of in this way. His ashes mingled with those of the Jews who had died there before him.

Bonhoeffer really believed that obeying God—even unto death—was the only way to live. And it was the only way to defeat evil. In his famous book *The Cost of Discipleship*, he wrote: "When Christ calls a man, he bids him come and die."[11] This was the life of faith in the God of the Scriptures. To accept the God of the Scriptures is to die to self, to embrace his eternal life in place of our own, and to henceforth banish all fear of death. For Bonhoeffer, this was the only way to live.

FIVE
Jackie Robinson

1919–72

Virtually every American boy is a baseball fan, and I was no exception. I grew up a mile from Shea Stadium and went to my first New York Mets game in 1970, when I was seven.

Many Brooklyn Dodgers fans were looking for a ball club to follow after the Dodgers abandoned Brooklyn for Los Angeles. Many of them became Mets fans.

Not far from Shea Stadium is Jackie Robinson Parkway, named after the great ballplayer who broke the color barrier in major-league baseball, so from a young age I was aware of Jackie Robinson. But what did I really know about him? Not much beyond the basics. But in 1998, when I was working for Chuck Colson, my colleague Roberto Rivera told me that Robinson was a Christian, and he pointed me to a new biography. I learned not only that Robinson was a Christian but also that his Christian faith was at the very center of his decision to accept Branch Rickey's invitation to play for the all-white Brooklyn Dodgers. I also learned that Branch Rickey himself was a Bible-thumping Methodist whose faith led him to find an African American ballplayer to break the color barrier.

How had I never heard any of this before? How come no one seemed to know this story—that at the center of one of the most important civil rights stories in America lay two men of passionate Christian faith?

◆ ◆ ◆

Jackie Roosevelt Robinson's story begins on January 31, 1919. He was born in Cairo, Georgia, the fifth child of the daughter of a former slave. Robinson's mother, Mallie Robinson, had admired former president Teddy Roosevelt, considering him a great leader, a devout Christian, and a fierce opponent of racism, so she named her son after him. Jackie's mother and his father, Jerry Robinson, were sharecroppers on a plantation owned by James Sasser, a white farmer, at a time when segregation ruled the South.

But the marriage between Jackie's parents was in bad shape by the time he was born, and his father left the family a few months later. Mallie knew that there was no future for her children in the South, and she secretly began to save money to move herself, her five children, and other family members to Pasadena, California. She did it secretly because white southerners often attempted to prevent blacks, who were a cheap source of labor, from leaving. The journey across the continent, in a Jim Crow train, took nine long days.

Mallie found employment as a domestic to a white family, and she worked hard to teach her children the value of "family, education, optimism, self-discipline, and above all, God."[1] She saw to it that her children were in church on Sunday and taught them the value of prayer.

Jackie's childhood years were not easy. The family was poor, his mother was away at work all day, and sometimes there was not enough to eat. As a young boy, Jackie helped the family by mowing lawns and selling hot dogs at ball games. Hostile white Pasadena neighbors tried to buy the Robinsons' house away from them and once even burned a cross in their yard. But Mallie Robinson's dignity, kindness, and hard work eventually won them over. Once, when Jackie and some friends retaliated for a white man's racial slur by spreading tar on his lawn, Mallie forced Jackie to repair the damage, supervising the repairs herself. Mallie believed in what the Bible taught, and the Bible taught that Christians were to bless those who persecuted them.

Jackie's extraordinary athletic talent and fierce competitiveness were apparent from an early age. At John Muir Technical High School, whether the sport was baseball, basketball, football, track and field, or tennis, Jackie excelled, lettering in four sports. At age seventeen, he participated in the Pacific Coast Negro Tennis Tournament, winning the junior boys singles championship.

But Jackie's older brother Mack was an even bigger star. He was such a gifted runner that the United States sent him to the 1936 Berlin Olympics, where he won the silver medal, right behind his teammate Jesse Owens! But on returning home, the triumphant national hero could find a job only as a street sweeper. To be sure, the great country whose Declaration of Independence states that "all men are created equal" was still a long way from any semblance of genuine racial equality.

◆ ◆ ◆

When Jackie enrolled at Pasadena Junior College (PJC) in 1937, his local fame as an athlete grew. Once again, he played football as a quarterback. Entering track and field events, Jackie even broke his famous brother's school broad jump record.

In the spring, baseball beckoned. After making the team, Jackie—who played shortstop and was the team's lead-off batter—made a name for himself by stealing bases.

By the time he left PJC, Jackie had racked up innumerable honors. He and two other black students were the first students of color to be elected to a school service organization called the Lancers. Jackie was elected (by the Kiwanis Clubs of Southern California) to the All-Southland Junior College Team for baseball. In 1938, he also became Pasadena Junior College's Most Valuable Player of the Year.

But racism continued to raise its ugly head during these Depression years. Restaurants and hotels often refused to serve Jackie and black teammates. Again and again Jackie was forced to endure these indignities and injustices, and he often struggled to control his temper.

On January 25, 1938, Jackie was arrested. That evening, he and a friend, Jonathan Nolan, were walking home from the movies when Nolan suddenly burst into song, singing "Flat Foot Floogie." In those days, "flat foot" was a less-than-flattering term for policemen, since most of them walked beats. A passing policeman overheard their tribute and decided to take offense; words were exchanged, and Jackie ended up spending the night in jail. A judge sentenced him to ten days, but because he knew Jackie was a football star, he suspended the sentence on the condition that Robinson avoid skirmishes with the police for two years.

A fellow PJC student named Hank Shatford recalled that the police "didn't regard Jack as a rabble-rouser. It's just that Jack would not take any stuff from them, and they knew it."[2]

One day, Jackie met a Methodist preacher named Karl Downs. Downs had a tremendous ability to inspire young people. He knew that Jackie was a Christian, and taught him that exploding in anger was not the Christian answer to injustice. But he also explained that a life truly dedicated to Christ was not submissive; on the contrary, it was heroic. Jackie's mother had taught her son the same thing, but now, coming from Karl Downs, it struck him in a new way.

Downs eventually led Jackie to a deeper faith in Jesus Christ, and Jackie brought his bad temper and fierce anger at injustices under control. He began to see that the path to justice would be won not with fists and fury but with love and restraint.

By then, Jackie was such a phenomenal baseball player that, had he been white, major-league clubs would have been fighting over him. But the major leagues rigidly enforced the rule against allowing black players on their teams. After leaving Pasadena Junior College without a degree, Jackie began considering college offers, ultimately deciding on UCLA. He was sure that UCLA coaches would use him to actually play instead of allow him to warm the bench as a token black.

But once at UCLA, Jackie decided against playing baseball. He announced he would take part only in football and track, partly because he wanted to concentrate on his studies, and partly because he hoped to follow in his brother Mack's footsteps—literally and figuratively—by being chosen for the US Olympic team.

But in July 1939, tragedy struck. Jackie's beloved brother Frank was killed when a car struck the motorcycle he was riding. A few weeks later, more trouble arrived in the form of a second racially tinged arrest. Jackie was driving his Plymouth home one evening with his friends riding on the running boards, when another car, driven by a white man, pulled up beside them at a stop. Dozens of young blacks crowded around, waiting to see what would happen, causing the white man to leave. When a motorcycle policeman pulled up, most of the crowd left. But suddenly the policeman pulled a gun on Jackie, pressing it into his stomach, and charged him with resisting arrest and hindering traffic. Jackie spent another night in jail, but pleaded not guilty to the charges. He was released on a twenty-five-dollar bond.

When UCLA officials caught wind of the arrest, they leaped into action, but mostly on their own behalf. In Jackie's absence, the judge found him guilty and fined him fifty dollars, which UCLA promptly paid. Jackie received his twenty-five-dollar bail money back, but he was annoyed at the guilty plea, along with the publicity the case received just as he was beginning a promising career at UCLA. Robinson recalled years later that this was his first real experience with vicious bigotry.

On the gridiron that year, "Jackrabbit Jackie Robinson" helped the UCLA football squad win game after game. And in the fall of 1940, Jackie met someone who would change his life: a seventeen-year-old freshman named Rachel Isum. Almost instantly Jackie knew he would marry the beautiful young nursing student, who shared his strong religious beliefs. UCLA's homecoming dance that year was held at the

Biltmore Hotel in Los Angeles. Jackie invited Rachel, and that night they danced to tunes like "Stardust" and "Mood Indigo."

As he and Rachel grew closer, Jackie continued his historic and attention-getting performance in college athletics. He became the first UCLA athlete to letter in four sports: football, baseball, basketball, and track. In 1940, he also won the NCAA Men's Outdoor Track and Field Championship in the long jump competition, leaping twenty-four feet five and a half inches. In basketball, Jackie won the individual league scoring title with 133 points, despite an injury to his hand; but, he was still not named to the All-League Cage Team. The *California Daily Bruin* cried foul in its March 5, 1941, issue, calling the vote a "flagrant bit of prejudice" and a "miscarriage of justice." That it was.

To the chagrin of his mother and Rachel, Jackie dropped out of UCLA just short of graduating, hoping to play professional football. But the black pro teams offered very little money. He then decided to take a job in Atascadero, California, as an athletic director with the National Youth Administration. But as it became increasingly clear that America would likely be joining the war in Europe, the teenagers were all sent home, and the job vanished.

Jackie next joined the Honolulu Bears, a semipro team with the Hawaii Senior Football League. The deal actually included construction work, for which Jackie was grateful, since he was eager to help his mother financially. Jackie played brilliant football, as he always had, but became disenchanted with the team. He also missed his family. On December 5, 1941, he left Hawaii for home aboard the *Lurline*. He left just in time. Two days later, as the ship steamed toward California, the Japanese attacked Pearl Harbor. Jackie was unaware of the attack and wondered why the ship's crew started painting the windows black. The ship, they told the passengers, would do everything possible to avoid enemy submarines.

While the war was bad news generally, in some cases it offered new job opportunities. For example, many African Americans were suddenly hired in defense industries that were previously closed to them. Jackie found a job at Lockheed Aircraft in Burbank, not far from his mother's home.

But the job did not last long. In March 1942, Jackie received his "Order to Report for Induction," and he traveled east to Kansas for basic training at Fort Riley. Jackie Roosevelt Robinson was now a member of Uncle Sam's segregated army. Despite becoming an expert marksman and passing the tests for Officer Candidate School, Jackie was turned down for officer training. The army instead put him in a segregated cavalry unit where he worked as a groom, looking after horses.

Robinson was furious, but the story didn't quite end there. It so happened that the heavyweight boxing champion of the world, Joe Louis himself was also stationed at Fort Riley. The world-famous boxer had enlisted as a soldier to help his country and boost morale. Robinson vented his frustrations to Louis, who decided to use his connections to improve the young man's situation. Louis contacted someone he knew in the White House, who in turn contacted someone else, and Robinson promptly received his officer's commission.

Jackie was appointed as morale officer for the black soldiers at Fort Hood, where he once again pushed the boundaries of segregation. For example, when black soldiers complained about how few stools there were for them at the post soda fountain, he looked into the matter, finding that there were just four for blacks (along the side of the fountain bordering the grill) compared to twelve for white soldiers along the front. Black soldiers and their families had to wait up to an hour to be served, even when seats for whites were empty.

Jackie phoned a Major Hafner to suggest that the number of seats for blacks be raised to six. Hafner, who assumed he was dealing with a white officer, objected; giving black soldiers access to seats in the front opened the possibility that one of them might sit down next to a white soldier or his wife.

"Lieutenant Robinson," Major Hafner said, "let me put it this way. Would you like it if your wife had to sit next to a nigger?"[3]

Robinson exploded into the phone. "I am a Negro officer!" he declared, adding some choice epithets for emphasis. Shortly thereafter, blacks visiting the soda fountain found two additional seats awaiting them.

Racism also showed up in army athletics. Jackie turned out for Fort Hood's baseball team, only to be told he would have to apply to the nonexistent colored team. An enraged Jackie walked off the field. Previously, at Fort Riley, he had been invited to join the football team only to be sent home on leave just prior to a game against the University of Missouri, which, Jackie later learned, refused to play against any team that included black players. An angry Jackie immediately resigned from the team. (Butt he was allowed to play table tennis, and in 1943 became the US Army's champion player!)

These experiences were minor compared to what the army had in store for Jackie in 1944. That June, Robinson traveled off base for a stay at McCloskey Hospital in Temple, Texas, so that his ankle could be examined. He had injured it during his years playing college football, and doctors were trying to ascertain whether he was fit to be deployed overseas with his unit—if not for combat, then as a morale officer.

On July 6, after spending time at the Negro officers' club, Jackie climbed aboard a Fort Hood bus to return to the hospital. He was heading for the rear of the bus when Jackie spotted Virginia Jones, the light-skinned wife of a fellow Fort Hood officer named Gordon Jones. She was seated four rows from the back.

A few blocks later, the driver noticed that Jackie was not sitting at the back of the bus and, furthermore, was sitting by a woman who appeared to be white. When he hollered back to him, "You got to move back, boy," Jackie refused.

The driver stopped the bus and tried again. He claimed that state law forbade allowing a black man to sit anywhere but the back of the bus, which Jackie knew was nonsense; the army forbade segregation on military buses. Jackie could sit anywhere he wanted. The driver angrily told Robinson that he would make trouble for him when they arrived at the post. Biographer Scott Simon writes: "White voices began to clamor, some telling Robinson to move, others calling for the driver to move on, let the boy be, they had places to go, just drive on and call the police when they stopped at the bus depot."[4]

Among the white riders making a fuss was a post kitchen employee who angrily informed Robinson that she intended to file charges against him. The bus driver asked Jackie for his identification card, which Robinson refused to provide. The driver told the other riders that "this nigger" was making trouble, and eventually the MPs were summoned.

When the military police arrived, they took Jackie to the guard room, where he engaged in several angry clashes with the officer of the day and the commander of the military police, Gerald Bear. Bear declared, "Lt. Robinson's attitude in general was disrespectful and impertinent to his superior officers, and very unbecoming to an officer in the presence of enlisted men."[5]

Jackie objected to this characterization of his behavior, but ultimately he was placed under arrest in quarters and driven back to the hospital. There, a friendly white doctor urged Jackie to undergo a blood test, as he had overheard a plan to accuse Jackie of being drunk and disorderly. Not surprisingly, since Jackie was a teetotaler, the test came back negative.

When Jackie told his senior officer, Lieutenant Colonel Paul Bates, about the incident, he discovered that Bear was planning to court-martial him. Since Colonel Bates refused to go along with this plan, Jackie was transferred to the 758th Tank Battalion, where a more obliging commander agreed to prosecute Robinson.

After his arrest, not trusting military lawyers to adequately represent him, Jackie turned to the National Association for the Advancement of Colored People (NAACP) for help. But the organization declined to assist him at the trial. In the end, Jackie asked that

First Lieutenant Robert Johnson serve as his individual counsel, and he later said that Johnson "did a great job on my behalf."[6]

Jackie was charged with "behaving with disrespect toward Capt. Gerald M. Bear, CMP, his superior officer," and of "willful disobedience of lawful command of Gerald M. Bear, CMP, his superior."[7]

The defense strategy was to "try to show that Robinson had not been insubordinate to Captain Bear but rather that Bear has managed the entire matter poorly," writes biographer Arnold Rampersad.[8] The strategy—which revealed, among other things, how many times Robinson had to listen to himself being described as a "nigger"—worked. Several character witnesses appeared on Jackie's behalf, including Colonel Bates, who told the court that Robinson was not only an outstanding soldier, but that he was also very respected by the enlisted men he worked with. In the end, a relieved Jackie was found not guilty of all charges by a panel made up of whites.

Jackie's deep religious faith helped him through this latest crisis. These difficult experiences may have been God's way of warming up Jackie for what he had planned for him later. They were, in effect, spiritual spring training for the even more difficult episodes that Jackie would face in the not-too-distant future.

Jackie was honorably discharged from the US Army on November 27, 1944. By then, he and Rachel were engaged, but with Jackie jobless, marriage would have to wait.

Although hardly a fan of segregation of any kind, much less in sports, Jackie accepted an offer to play for the Kansas City Monarchs, a Negro National League team. He also fielded an offer from his old friend Karl Downs, now president of the Samuel Huston College in Austin, Texas. Downs invited Jackie to teach physical education at the college, and Jackie accepted, dramatically improving the college's athletic program and becoming a popular figure with students.

As he thought about his future with Rachel and considered what might lie ahead for them, Jackie never could have dreamed of anything close to the reality that was about to occur. His life was soon to change dramatically. A war was then raging in the sports pages around the country about whether major-league baseball should be integrated. And far away from Jackie, in the distant East Coast city of New York, in the borough of Brooklyn, an idea was brewing that would catapult him into the national consciousness—and into American history.

It all began with a colorful sixty-four-year-old figure named Branch Rickey. Rickey was the legendary general manager of the Brooklyn Dodgers team. Rickey was an energetic and relentless innovator whose ideas had already changed baseball in many ways we now take for granted, including use of the batting helmet, batting cages, pitching machines, and statistical analysis. Rickey is even credited with inventing the farm system of the minor leagues and with creating the first spring training facility. But what he was about to do would eclipse all of these things. That's because as far as Branch Rickey was concerned, the national pastime had to be integrated. And he thought that he was the one to bring about the integration. The only questions were, how should he go about it, and who should be the first black player?

Rickey, a devout Christian who refused to play or attend games on Sunday, knew he would have to be very careful as he proceeded. Other baseball owners and managers would be dead set against the idea of integrating baseball, as would many players. But Rickey's deep Christian faith told him that injustice must be fought wherever one found it. As he saw it, the Jim Crow laws that excluded black players from baseball were intolerably unjust. Rickey considered that his past experiences and his position in the game had set him up to do something profoundly important for the sport. Indeed, he saw in all of this "a chance to intervene in the moral history of the nation, as Lincoln had done."[9]

Rickey took seriously Jesus' command that we be "wise as serpents." So, very quietly, he sent scouts to Negro League ball games. To disguise his intentions, Rickey announced that he planned to start a new Negro club to be called the Brooklyn Brown Dodgers. Who could argue with that?

After he reviewed scouting reports, Rickey's attention focused on one particular player, then with the Kansas City Monarchs. According to biographer Scott Simon, Rickey believed that Jackie Robinson had everything he was looking for: Robinson "could run, hit with power, and field with grace. He could steal bases and bunt shrewdly, and he excelled in the game's mental aspects. He was a college man, a veteran, a world-caliber athlete, and a dark, handsome, round-shouldered man with a shy smile."[10]

Perhaps even more important, Rickey saw that Robinson had plenty of experience playing with white players and that—like Rickey—he was a serious Bible-believing Christian with a strong moral character. In the struggle that lay ahead, these characteristics would be crucial. He felt strongly that if the person he chose for this extraordinary task could be goaded into saying the wrong thing or appearing in any way less than noble and dignified, the press would have a field day and the whole project would go up in flames. What was worse, if that were to happen, the whole idea of integrating baseball would likely be set back another ten or fifteen years. Rickey had to be sure he was choosing someone who understood the tremendous import of not fighting back, despite what he would hear—and he would hear plenty. But in the end, he felt he had found the man for the job. It was time for him to meet Jackie Robinson.

That was why, in August 1945, less than three weeks after the explosion of atomic bombs over Hiroshima and Nagasaki effectively ended America's war with Japan, Clyde Sukeforth caught a train to Chicago to talk with Jackie, who was playing with the Monarchs in Comiskey Park. Leaning over the third-base railing, Sukeforth called out to Robinson. He said he was there on behalf of Branch Rickey, who was starting a new team, the Brooklyn Brown Dodgers. Sukeforth asked Jackie to throw a few balls so that he could assess his arm strength. To Jackie it all seemed a bit odd and mysterious.

"Why is Mr. Rickey interested in my arm?" he asked. "Why is he interested in *me*?"[11]

Sukeforth's cryptic response only deepened the mystery: he told Robinson to meet him after the game at the Stevens Hotel. When Jackie arrived, he fired more questions at Sukeforth. The talent scout couldn't say very much—after all, he was on a stealth mission—but his answers were enough to convince Jackie to agree to accompany him to New York and meet Branch Rickey.

A few days later, on August 28, Sukeforth and Jackie met at the Brooklyn Dodgers' headquarters on Montague Street in Brooklyn Heights. Though far from the Jim Crow South, there was still a whites-only elevator in the building. Sukeforth slipped the elevator boy the then princely sum of two dollars to look the other way so that he and Jackie could ride up together to the fourth floor to Rickey's office. Jackie was about to meet the man who would not only change his life but also become like a father to him.

According to Sukeforth, the air in the room when Rickey and Robinson met was electric. At first Rickey and Jackie just stared at each other. Rickey stared because he knew what was at stake and why the moment was potentially historic. The young man before him might well become a historic figure, and this scene might well be written about in future books. For his part, Jackie had no idea what was happening or why Rickey was staring at him. And as Jackie wasn't about to be stared at without staring back, he stared back. What he saw was a pudgy, bespectacled man with bushy eyebrows, a bow tie, and a cigar. The staring continued.

Then Rickey suddenly asked Jackie if he had a girlfriend. It was a bizarre way to start the conversation, Jackie thought, but then again, the whole affair had been strange from the beginning. Rickey made it clear that Jackie might face real challenges ahead, and the love of a good woman—of a good wife—would be very important. Jackie still didn't understand, and his face showed it.

"Do you know why you were brought here?" Rickey asked Robinson.

"Sure," Robinson replied, "to play on the new Brooklyn Brown Dodgers team."

"No," Rickey said. "That isn't it. You were brought here, Jackie, to play for the Brooklyn organization. Perhaps on Montreal to start with, and—"

"Me? Play for Montreal?" Jackie was stunned. The implications were impossible to take in so quickly.

"If you can make it, yes. Later on—also if you can make it—you'll have a chance with the Brooklyn Dodgers."

What Rickey was saying seemed impossible. Jackie was speechless.

Rickey continued to spin out his long-held fantasy. "I want to win the pennant and we need ball players!" he roared, pounding his desk. "Do you think you can do it?"

There was a long pause while Jackie thought it over. Finally he answered: "Yes."

When Rickey asked Jackie if he was up to the job, he wasn't talking only about playing great baseball. He knew Jackie could do that. What he meant, he explained, was that if Jackie were to become major-league baseball's first black player, he would be in for a tremendous amount of abuse, both verbal and physical.

Jackie said he was sure he could face up to whatever came his way. He wasn't afraid of anyone and had been in any number of fistfights over the years when anyone had challenged him.

But Rickey had something else in mind. "I know you're a good ball-player," Rickey said. "What I don't know is whether you have the guts." Rickey knew he meant something dramatically different from what Robinson was thinking, so he continued. "I'm looking," Rickey said, "for a ballplayer with guts enough *not to fight back*."[12]

This was an unexpected wrinkle, to put it mildly.

Rickey then spun out a number of scenarios to convey what he meant, in the form of a dramatic pop quiz. Biographer Arnold Rampersad writes,

Rickey stripped off his coat and enacted out a variety of parts that portrayed examples of an offended Jim Crow. Now he was a white hotel clerk rudely refusing Jack accommodations; now a supercilious white waiter in a restaurant; now a brutish railroad conductor. He became a foul-mouthed opponent, Jack recalled, talking about "my race, my parents, in language that was almost unendurable." Now he was a vengeful base runner, vindictive spikes flashing in the sun, sliding into Jack's black flesh—"How do you like that, nigger boy?"[13]

According to Rickey, not only would Robinson have to tolerate such abuse, but he would need to be almost superhuman and to commit himself to never, ever hit back. This was at the heart of the whole enterprise. If Jackie could promise that, then he and Rickey could make it work. They could open the doors for other black players and change the game forever.

Jackie knew that resisting the urge to fight back really would require a superhuman effort, but he was deeply moved by Rickey's vision. He thought of his mother. He thought of all the black people who deserved someone to break this ground for them, even if it was difficult. He believed God had chosen him for this noble purpose. He believed he *had* to do it—for black kids, for his mother, for his wife, for himself.

Knowing that Jackie shared his Christian faith and wanting to reinforce the spiritual dimensions of what the two men were about to embark on, Rickey brought out a copy of a book titled *Life of Christ* by Giovanni Papini. He flipped to the passage in which Papini discusses the Sermon on the Mount and refers to it as "the most stupefying of [Jesus'] revolutionary teachings." It certainly was revolutionary. In fact, it seemed impossible. In Matthew 5:38–41, Jesus said,

> Ye have heard that it hath been said, An eye for an eye, and a tooth for a tooth: But I say unto you, That ye resist not evil: But whosoever shall smite thee on thy right cheek, turn to him the other also. And

if any man will sue thee at the law, and take away thy coat, let him
have thy cloak also. And whosoever shall compel thee to go a mile,
go with him twain. (KJV)

Rickey was betting that Jackie Robinson knew what he himself
knew: although this was indeed humanly impossible, with God's help
it was entirely possible. And Jackie did know it. As a Christian, he knew
that if he committed himself to doing this thing—which both men felt
was God's will—God would give Jackie the strength to accomplish it.

So Jackie Roosevelt Robinson and Branch Rickey shook hands.
And there, in that fourth-floor office in Brooklyn to which Jackie had
ridden in a whites-only elevator, under a portrait of Abraham Lincoln,
history was made. It was a momentous day not only for baseball but
for America.

Jackie was now contractually bound to the Brooklyn Dodgers, but
this fact had to remain a secret for the present. All who knew of it
had to be sworn to secrecy if this noble and daring experiment were
to succeed.

Two months later—on October 23—in Montreal, Jackie at last
broke his silence and shocked the world by signing a contract to play
with the Montreal Royals. When the press besieged him with questions, Jackie answered, "Of course, I can't begin to tell you how happy I
am that I am the first member of my race in organized baseball. I realize how much it means to me, my race, and to baseball. I can only say
I'll do my very best to come through in every manner."[14]

For his part, Branch Rickey disingenuously insisted that he simply
wanted to win pennants. "If an elephant could play center field better
than any man I have, I would play the elephant," he claimed.[15]

Some—including New York Giants president Horace Stoneham—
applauded Rickey's decision, while others, including many in the press,
vehemently attacked it. But it was settled. Next spring, Jackie Robinson

would be the first black player in what had been whites-only professional baseball since the 1880s.

In preparation that winter, Jackie went on a ten-week barnstorming tour of Venezuela. Before he began playing for Montreal that spring, Jackie would do something else that was important and momentous. He would marry Rachel. He traveled to California to do just that, and on February 10, 1946, they were married by Jackie's friend Karl Downs in a big traditional wedding at the Independent Church of Christ. The couple honeymooned in San Jose, but the wedding trip was cut short by Jackie's need to begin spring training at the Dodgers' camp in Daytona Beach, Florida. Rachel went with her new husband, and for the first time in her life she witnessed the segregation laws and attitudes of the Jim Crow South. In New Orleans, they were bumped from their next flight and the one after that, too, with no explanation. The couple could not find an airport restaurant to serve them. After spending the night in a filthy hotel room, Jackie and Rachel were finally allowed to fly to Pensacola—where once again they were kept off their next plane, evidently because white passengers wanted their seats. Deciding to take a bus to Jacksonville, the newlyweds were ordered to the uncomfortable seats in the back, where they spent sixteen miserable hours.

"I had a bad few seconds, deciding whether I could continue to endure this humiliation," Robinson wrote later.

The couple were bumped off their flight again in Pensacola, angering Robinson further. But he drew the line at making a scene, because he knew it would only result in newspaper headlines and even possibly arrest for the couple. And giving in to rage might have meant the end of his major-league career even before it began.

In addition, as he and Rachel prepared for the ordeals that would come with Jackie's promotion, they "agreed that I had no right to lose my temper and jeopardize the chances of all the blacks who would follow me if I could help break down the barriers."[16]

Another sixteen-hour bus ride finally brought the couple to Daytona.

Despite a rocky few weeks, by the end of the training camp, Robinson was officially invited to become part of the Royals team, which meant moving to Montreal. Jackie and Rachel had no idea what to expect about racial attitudes there, but they soon discovered to their great surprise that the French-speaking people in their neighborhood could not have been friendlier. By now Rachel was expecting the couple's first baby—Jackie Roosevelt Robinson Jr.—and the neighborhood women brought her advice and ration book coupons so she could buy the healthy food she needed.

Jackie's first game in a Montreal uniform took place on April 18, 1946, at Roosevelt Stadium in Jersey City, New Jersey. That day Jackie officially broke the fabled color line in professional baseball. And his athletic performance could hardly have been better. Jackie got four hits, including a three-run homer, scored four times, and drove in three runs. He even stole two bases. The Royals trounced their opponents 14–1.

To be fair, Jackie's talents on the diamond had never been in question. Far more important was whether he could keep his promise not to respond to the racial ugliness that would surely rear its head in the coming weeks. As Rickey had predicted, Jackie quickly became the regular target of vicious name-calling and race-baiting. But with God's help, Jackie was able to stay above the fray and avoid responding in kind, despite the tremendous temptation to do so.

Throughout that summer, Jackie showed himself to be a man of truly rare character. Anyone with eyes to see could see that Jackie's not fighting back against such filth and injustice was as heroic an accomplishment as anything the sports world had ever witnessed. And if that wasn't enough, his performance on the field continued to stagger the naysayers. That first season he was among the very best players—if not the single best player—in the now-integrated minor league. His batting average was .349, a team record, and he won the league's batting crown, the first Montreal player ever to do so. With Jackie's help, the Royals that season won one hundred games, the most in team history, and they won the pennant by a stunning eighteen and a half games. In every way, Jackie Robinson had magnificently vindicated Branch Rickey's historic decision.

After the season, Jackie returned to Los Angeles to witness the birth of his son. He waited all through the winter for the call he hoped would finally come, inviting him to Brooklyn and, at long last, into baseball's major leagues.

That call came early on April 10, 1947, from Rickey's secretary to Robinson, who was staying in a Manhattan hotel. Could Jackie come immediately to a meeting with Rickey? It all happened with lightning speed. Later that day, while the Dodgers were in the sixth inning of a game, one of Rickey's assistants began handing out press releases to sports reporters in the press box. They announced that the Brooklyn Dodgers had just purchased the contract of Jackie Robinson from the Montreal Royals.

In the Dodgers' dressing room that day, Jackie was given a uniform with the number 42 on the back. Putting it on, he posed and smiled for photographs. The following day, Jackie reported to Ebbets Field to meet with Clyde Sukeforth.

"Robinson, how are you feeling today?"[17]

"Fine," answered Jackie.

"Okay," Sukeforth said, "then you're playing first base for us today against the Yankees."

"I just sorta gulped," Jackie recalled.

Sadly, many opponents of what Robinson and Rickey were trying to achieve showed up at Dodgers' games and loudly expressed their opinions. Worse yet, some of them *played* in Dodgers' games. Just twelve days after the Dodgers signed Jackie, the Dodgers were playing the Philadelphia Phillies at Ebbets Field. During this game, Robinson was subjected to vicious abuse by none other than Phillies manager Ben Chapman, who also encouraged several players to mistreat Robinson.

Jackie remembered the pain many years later in his autobiography. "Starting to the plate in the first inning, I could scarcely believe my ears," he wrote.

Almost as if it had been synchronized by some demonic conductor, hate poured forth from the Phillies dugout.

"Hey, nigger, why don't you go back to the cotton field where you belong?"

"They're waiting for you in the jungles, black boy!"

"Hey, snowflake, which one of those white boys' wives are you dating tonight?"[18]

The next day was just as bad. It was profoundly ugly. In fact, much of what was said was much worse, and is unprintable here. Of course, when he heard all of this, Jackie was strongly tempted to go back on his word to Branch Rickey. But he held his tongue and his temper. Instead, he stoically walked to the plate without favoring the Philadelphia bench with so much as a glance.

Ironically, the flood of filth from Chapman had an unexpectedly positive result: it so infuriated Jackie's teammates that it put all of them on Robinson's side, once and for all. Until that point, a number of the Dodgers players had been none too keen about playing alongside a black man. But what they saw that day changed everything forever. Second-baseman Eddie Stanky spoke for the whole team when he shouted at the opposing dugout: "Listen, you yellow-bellied cowards, why don't you yell at somebody who can answer back?"[19]

Branch Rickey was delighted with the team's response. Chapman's evil intentions had, he said, "solidified and unified thirty men, not one of whom was willing to sit by and see someone kick around a man who had his hands tied behind his back."[20]

Yet the abuse continued from other sources. On the road, hotels and restaurants refused service to Jackie, forcing him to eat and sleep away from the team. Letters arrived, containing death threats. Players on other teams kicked Jackie, stepped on his feet, struck him on the head with pitches, and even slashed painfully at his leg with their spikes, one time creating a seven-inch gash in his leg. Despite all of it, Jackie kept his cool—and his promise to Rickey. And he kept his reliance on God, getting down on his knees every night to pray for strength.

That season, Jackie played in 151 games and somehow he got through all of them without a single incident of retaliation. By the end of the 1947 season, Jackie Robinson had become one of the most famous men in America. And once again, his performance on the field spoke as loudly as anything. He was voted 1947 Rookie of the Year. His batting average was .297; he had amassed an amazing 175 hits and had scored 125 runs; and he had even led the league in sacrifices and stolen bases.[21]

His numbers the following year were again spectacular. But the abuse continued. At one game in Cincinnati, when spectators in the stands were shouting racist comments at Robinson, his teammate Pee Wee Reese pointedly walked over to him and put his arm around him, as though to say to the bigots in the crowd, "if you are against him, you're against all of us." It was a signature moment, and a statue commemorating it stands today in Brooklyn's minor-league KeySpan Park.

In 1949, Jackie exceeded everyone's already high expectations by putting up a batting average of .342, with 124 RBIs, 122 runs scored, and 37 stolen bases. He even started at second base during that year's All-Star Game. At the end of the season, he won the National League's MVP Award. Anyone who doubted whether this man was a great baseball player had to put those doubts aside. And anyone who ever doubted whether he could withstand the torrent of abuse that came against him had to do the same. Branch Rickey knew that his difficult and noble experiment had been a resounding success.

I n 1948, several other black players were invited to play in the major leagues, taking some of the pressure off Jackie. Gradually the level of invective tailed off, and Jackie could concentrate on simply being a spectacular baseball player. His 1949 stats were so impressive that the Dodgers raised his salary to $35,000, at the time a grand sum and the highest salary ever paid to any player in the franchise. Jackie's fame was now such that Count Basie recorded a hit song titled "Did You See Jackie Robinson Hit That Ball?" and in 1950 Hollywood produced the feature film *The Jackie Robinson Story*. As was often done in biopics of that period, Jackie was hired to play himself in the film.

Business opportunities began to come his way, and Jackie got involved with many charitable groups, especially those that helped children of both races. During these years as a player for the Dodgers, Robinson began to challenge hotels and restaurants that still discriminated against black ballplayers, with the result that a number of them dropped their segregationist policies.

And his success as a ballplayer continued. In 1950, Robinson led the league in double plays for a second baseman, and in 1951, he did it again. That year, his outstanding talents as a player almost carried the Dodgers into the World Series, but the crushing defeat of Bobby Thompson's famous "Shot Heard 'Round the World" home run took them out of contention. The next year, 1952, Jackie and the Dodgers brought victory—and bedlam—to Brooklyn when they won the National League pennant, although they eventually lost in the World Series to the Yankees in seven games. In 1953, Jackie batted .329 and led Brooklyn to another National League pennant, but the Dodgers again lost the World Series to the Yankees, this time in six games. In 1954 the team didn't win the pennant; but at last, in 1955, the Dodgers won the pennant again and then went on to take the World Series in seven games from their Bronx rivals.

Winning the World Series was a high-water mark for Robinson. But age was beginning to take its toll on his performance: his average that year dipped to a career low of .256.

The following year marked Jackie's tenth anniversary as a Dodger. It was also the year he began exhibiting the effects of undiagnosed diabetes, and at the end of the season, the Dodgers opted to trade him to the New York Giants.

With his body wearing down, the thirty-eight-year-old baseball legend had already decided he'd had enough baseball and announced his retirement from the game. Even before the Dodgers traded him, he had decided to take a job with the Chock Full O'Nuts company, where he would serve as vice president for personnel. He would never play for the archrival Giants.

In an article he wrote for *Look* magazine, Jackie said: "I'll miss the excitement of baseball, but now I'll be able to spend more time with my family." His three children, Jackie, Sharon, and David, would now "have a real father they can play with and talk to in the evening and every weekend. They won't have to look for him on TV."[22]

Always interested in helping the poor, Jackie now formed the Jackie Robinson Construction Company, dedicated to building low-income housing. He regularly bought food for the needy, leaving it at food banks for distribution. He visited sick children in hospitals and crusaded against drug use, which his son Jackie had struggled with. He also became deeply involved in the burgeoning civil rights movement, working with Martin Luther King Jr. and traveling to the Deep South in an effort to bring about full freedom for the descendants of slaves. Robinson also became the first black analyst for ABC's *Major League Baseball Game of the Week* program and became a board member of the NAACP.

In 1962, the forty-three-year-old icon was voted into the Baseball Hall of Fame—the first black player to be so honored. Almost unbelievably, it had been just fifteen years since blacks had been allowed to play in the major leagues. Yet in that same year, as Robinson sadly noted in an essay, University of Mississippi students rioted as African American James Meredith attempted to enroll at Ole Miss. To use a phrase from Winston Churchill, Jackie's admission to baseball's Hall of Fame was not the beginning of the end of America's toxic racial battles, "but merely the end of the beginning."

I n more and more ways, Jackie's body began letting him down. He suffered severe pains in his legs and feet, the legacy of the years spent playing football, basketball, and baseball. He suffered mild heart attacks in 1968 and 1970 and was diagnosed with diabetes and hypertension. Blood vessels ruptured in his eyes, which led to the loss of much of his vision.

In June 1971, Robinson's troubled older son, Jackie Jr., was killed in a car accident at the age of twenty-four. Those who knew Jackie felt that after all he had been through over the years, this was the hardest blow of all.

On October 15, 1972, just one week before his death, Jackie Robinson and his family gathered at Riverfront Stadium in Cincinnati where Jackie threw out the first ceremonial pitch during Game Two of the World Series. As tens of thousands of Pirates and Reds fans watched, the baseball icon graciously accepted a plaque marking the twenty-fifth anniversary of his debut with the Dodgers, and then, his voice shaking with the emotion of the day, the man who'd broken baseball's color barrier said, "I'd like to live to see a black manager, I'd like to live to see the day when there is a black man coaching at third base."[23]

There were still civil rights battles to be fought, but Jackie would not live to see them waged and won. On the morning of October 24, 1972, Rachel was fixing breakfast when Jackie raced from the bedroom to the kitchen. Putting his arms around his wife of twenty-six years, Jackie said, "I love you," and collapsed. He died of a heart attack in an ambulance headed to the hospital. He was just fifty-three.

A few days later, Jackie's funeral took place at New York's Riverside Church before twenty-five hundred mourners. Tens of thousands of people lined the streets as Jackie was taken to Cypress Hills Cemetery, where he was buried next to his son and namesake.

The intervening years have brought even greater recognition not only of what Jackie Robinson did but also of who he was: a man of character and courage, dignity and faith. In 1984, President Ronald Reagan posthumously awarded Jackie the Medal of Freedom, America's highest civilian honor. In April 1997, President Bill Clinton joined fifty-four thousand Mets fans at Shea Stadium to celebrate the fiftieth anniversary of Jackie's breaking the color barrier in the major leagues. Robinson's grandson Jesse threw out the ceremonial pitch, and Baseball Commissioner Bud Selig announced that major-league baseball would retire Robinson's number. "Number 42 belongs to Jackie Robinson for the ages," he said, and the crowd roared.[24]

In 1999, twenty-seven years after his death, Robinson was named to major-league baseball's All-Century Team.

Usually, when considering the life and career of a baseball player, we tote up his statistics and compare them to the statistics of those who have gone before. But how can we tally what an achievement it was to endure what Jackie Robinson endured those first few years? It was an incalculable and heroic sacrifice that can never be reckoned or understood by any conventional standards. Robinson did what he agreed to do when he met that day with Branch Rickey, and he changed the game forever. It was a singular feat of such great moral strength that all athletic strength must pale in comparison. With God's help, one man lifted up a whole people and pulled a whole nation into the future.

January 31, 2019, will mark Jackie Robinson's one hundredth birthday. There will surely be many memorials around the world. But I hope the world will not forget the heart of the Jackie Robinson story, that he changed America by successfully living out, both on and off the baseball field, the revolutionary and world-changing words of Jesus:

> Ye have heard that it hath been said, An eye for an eye, and a tooth for a tooth: But I say unto you, That ye resist not evil: But whosoever shall smite thee on thy right cheek, turn to him the other also. And if any man will sue thee at the law, and take away thy coat, let him have thy cloak also. And whosoever shall compel thee to go a mile, go with him twain.

SIX
Pope John Paul II

1920–2005

The new pope was the subject of the news everywhere during the last week of August in 1978. I was a fifteen-year-old, about to enter my junior year in high school in Danbury, Connecticut. Although I had many Catholic friends, I was raised Greek Orthodox, so I took little real interest in anything having to do with who was or wasn't the pope. But it was impossible to be unaware of the events transpiring in Rome at that time. It was very big news, and I could understand why, since there were almost a billion Catholics around the world.

Besides, there was never a new pope. As far back as I could remember, the pope had always been Pope Paul VI. This was a given, and not something I thought could ever change, in the same way that the Queen of England was always Queen Elizabeth and, as I write this book, is still Queen Elizabeth. Not many things transcend election cycles, but popes and English monarchs are two that do. So until that fall, when the news was awash with this monumental change, I didn't think change was possible. I remembered once hearing about the pope before Pope Paul. His name was Pope John, but that papacy ended before I was born and, as far as I was concerned, might as well have been during the Middle Ages. So for me, there was only one pope in the world. And suddenly all that changed.

The new pope, Albino Luciani of Venice, took the name Pope John Paul, and since he was the first pope in two thousand years who had the name John Paul, he was officially Pope John Paul I. So that was settled. But no sooner had the news about the new pope died down than there was new news that the newly named pope had died. This was on September 28, just thirty-three days after he had become pope. And so, one month after a pope had died and the College of Cardinals had elected a new pope once more, that new pope died, and they would have to elect a second new pope. It was all quite out of the ordinary, to say the least. Once again the world focused its attention on what was happening in the Vatican. In a way you began to hope that whomever they picked would be reasonably young and healthy.

As it turned out, he was. The man who was now chosen by the College of Cardinals was named Karol Wojtyla, and amazingly he was only fifty-eight years old, practically a teenager by historical papal standards. What's more, he was said to be especially youthful and athletic for his age. And oh, yes, he was from Poland. To almost everyone, the idea of a non-Italian pope was a bit surprising, almost as surprising as if the cardinals had chosen a Protestant. It had been 456 years since the last non-Italian pope began his papacy. A Dutchman, Adrian VI, was elected in 1522. So yes, it had been a while. To put things in perspective, Pope Adrian was a rough contemporary of Christopher Columbus.

This was all very big news on many levels. And there was more. This new pope was said to speak twelve languages and to have written plays and poetry and to have studied philosophy. He was an avid sportsman, who loved soccer and who hiked, weight-trained, swam, and jogged. Had I heard that correctly? A pope who weight-trained and jogged? Even in the 1970s, when it seemed that everyone was jogging, the idea of a pope doing such a thing was almost unthinkable.

Out of respect to his short-lived predecessor, John Paul I, the new pope chose the name John Paul II, which occasionally came to be abbreviated as JP2. Even that seemed young and contemporary. And the more one saw and heard of him, the more extraordinary it all seemed. There was a friendliness, a sunniness, and an optimism to this man that were tremendously refreshing. How was it that his election could somehow stir even non-Catholics? What was it about him that seemed to represent hope? He was supremely serious about God, but he didn't come across as dour or "religious" in the negative sense. He seemed fun and full of life.

So yes, the election of this new pope was big news in a few ways, even to a non-Catholic teenager.

But as the years passed I realized that this pope was more than merely young and non-Italian. He was different in many ways. Before the attempt on his life and before Parkinson's disease slowed him down, he was extraordinarily active and vigorous, traveling the world almost constantly, eventually visiting some 129 countries, beaming at crowds, and drawing vast numbers of young people to the faith.

He was even brave and heroic, traveling to Poland, where he publicly stood up to the Communists there and encouraged the fledgling Solidarity movement. And we cannot forget that he was shot by an assassin and almost died—and later met with the man who tried to kill him and forgave him. It was all like something out of a movie.

So who was this spectacularly gifted man, suddenly now the supreme pontiff? Who was this heroic figure who had once acted in plays, but who would play a lead role in a compelling real-life drama in modern history, the battle between freedom and communism?

Of all the great men in this book, there is only one who has come to be called "the Great." John Paul the Great. Let's find out who he was.

◆ ◆ ◆

The man who became Pope John Paul II was born Karol Wojtyla on May 18, 1920, in Wadowice, Poland. (The name Karol is another form of the English Charles.) The boy's father, Karol Sr., was an army clerk, and his mother, Emilia, was a part-time seamstress and former teacher. The family lived close to the local church, and as both parents were devout Catholics, little Karol—or Lolek, as he was nicknamed—was there every day.

Lolek was the youngest of three children born to his parents. Edmund was fourteen years older, but Lolek's sister died before Lolek was born. Lolek's mother was quite sickly throughout his childhood, suffering from heart and kidney disease, so the bulk of the parenting fell to his father, Karol Sr. In their book *John Paul II: A Tribute in Words and Pictures*, Monsignor Virgilio Levi and Christine Allison write:

> The Wojtylas were like most Catholic Poles; their home contained the symbols of their faith—crucifixes, a painting of the Blessed Mary, and holy water in a vessel by the door. Lolek wore the scapular he received at First Communion every single day. . . . But faith in the Wojtyla home went deeper: it was embodied in the human heart. Karol Sr. lived a life of simple Christian humility. "Almost all of the memories of childhood are connected with my father," Lolek would write, years later, as pope. "His example alone was sufficient to inculcate discipline and a sense of duty."

The image of his father on his knees in prayer would never leave Karol Wojtyla. And the world would often see him in precisely this pose, too, whether kissing the soil as he landed in a foreign country or at his more usual place of prayer at Saint Peter's in Rome.

When Lolek was just eight, his mother died. It was only the beginning of a number of tragedies that would befall the boy. Four years later, when Lolek was twelve, his beloved brother, Edmund, died of scarlet fever. Despite their differences in age, Edmund and Lolek were close, and young Lolek was devastated by the loss. Years later he wrote, "My mother's death made a deep impression . . . and my brother's perhaps a still deeper one because of the dramatic circumstances in which it occurred and because I was more mature."[1] His brother's death forced him to grow up quickly, and without question it drove him closer to God. The quiet, devout boy now became even more devout, spending more of his time in church and in prayer.

Lolek had a brilliant mind and did very well in school. But despite his serious devotion to God and his studiousness, he was a rather typical teenager of his time. For one thing, he was athletic and an avid soccer player. During his high school years, he was passionate about the theater, acting in and even directing and producing plays presented by the Wadowice Theater Circle.

As valedictorian of his high school class, Lolek delivered a speech at the commencement exercises. The archbishop of Krakow, Adam Sapieha, was present that day as the primary speaker. The brilliant young teenager's speech so impressed the visiting cleric that he took the opportunity to inquire whether Karol was considering attending seminary. When the young man replied that he was not, the archbishop was deeply disappointed.

After high school, Karol enrolled in the Jagiellonian University in Krakow. Established in 1364, this was one of the world's oldest universities, and there Karol continued to excel, studying philology and numerous languages. He was also a volunteer librarian and was active in the theater, both as an actor and as a playwright.

Despite all his activities, Karol kept up his daily church attendance and devotions. In this way he was certainly atypical of other students with whom he spent much of his time, and it's hard to know what they made of their profoundly Christian friend and classmate. In his book *Great Souls: Six Who Changed the Century*, David Aikman tells us that "on one occasion, as a practical joke, his classmates placed a note on his desk that read, 'Karol Wojtyla, Apprentice Saint.'"[2]

During these years in Poland, the culture around Karol was in a state of turmoil. For one thing, anti-Semitism, which had already reached monstrous levels in Germany under Hitler, was now making its way into Poland as well. But Karol's upbringing would set him in serious opposition to all of it. His hometown, Wadowice, was one-third Jewish, and the Catholic and Jewish communities there coexisted amicably. The Wojtyla family had always had many Jewish friends with whom their lives were intertwined. One close Jewish friend of Karol's was Jerzy Kluger. In fact, Kluger and Karol remained lifelong friends. When many years later Kluger settled in Rome as an adult, his family treated their old friend—then living in Rome as Pope John Paul II—as one of their own.

Despite this growing anti-Semitism in Krakow, young Karol stood up for the Jews whenever he could. Yet like most Poles then—indeed, like most Europeans—he failed to grasp the seriousness of the worsening situation, even when Jewish friends were forced to leave the country.

Regardless of the turmoil, this period represented a calm and mostly studious time in the life of Karol Wojtyla. That calm was shattered dramatically, however, on September 1, 1939, the day the Nazis attacked Poland. All that terrible month, Hitler's Luftwaffe rained hell from the skies while ruthless SS troops murdered Polish soldiers and civilians alike on the ground. By November the country called Poland had officially ceased to exist and—thanks to the Hitler-Stalin pact—it was occupied by both the Nazis and the Soviets. What happened to the Polish people during this era has been much written about, and it is among the saddest periods in the history of any nation. Millions of Poles would be killed in the months and years ahead. Among those rounded up and deported as the Nazis took over were 186 professors from Jagiellonian University, which soon shut its doors.

Doing his best to cope with his circumstances, Karol found work first as a delivery boy and then as a quarry worker to support himself and his father, who was living with him in Krakow. He was later transferred to the Solvay chemical plant. Throughout those years, Karol kept his mind and soul fed through reading, having religious discussions and debates with coworkers, participating in clandestine theatrical activities, and praying. In his magisterial biography, *Witness to Hope*, George Weigel writes:

Fellow workers . . . remember Karol Wojtyla praying on his knees at the Borek Falecki plant, unafraid of ridicule and seemingly able to tune out the racket around him to concentrate on his conversation with God. On his way home . . . he frequently stopped at the parish in Podgorze run by the Redemptorist priests, to pray or to attend early morning Mass after completing the night shift. "From here," he recalled thirty years later, "I gained the strength to last through the difficult times of the years of Occupation."[3]

Karol was greatly helped and guided during these years by an unassuming man named Jan Leopold Tyranowski, whom Karol met at his parish church. Tyranowski was a tailor, not a clergyman, but he was a deeply spiritual layman who participated in a discipleship program called the Living Rosary, created to help Polish youth remain dedicated to their faith during the war years. Meeting with young men both in groups and individually, Tyranowski was a spiritual director who had a significant impact on their lives.

Karol would always remember Tyranowski's teachings on suffering and how it can draw us closer to God. After becoming pope, he recalled the humble tailor as "one of those unknown saints, hidden like a marvelous light at the bottom of life, at a depth where night usually reigns." In him young Karol had seen "the beauty of the soul opened up by grace."[4]

The years of occupation and the manual labor they brought with them taught him something else besides. They "introduced him," as Weigel puts it, "to a world he had never known before, the world of the industrial laborer."[5] In this world he learned new lessons about the dignity of labor and of those who performed it. The lessons would serve him well in the years to come.

In the meantime, one of the greatest blows yet was about to befall the young Karol. One night he arrived home with food and medicine for his father, only to discover that the sixty-two-year-old man had died. The son was devastated and spent the whole night in prayer beside his father's body. Though a friend had come to stay with him, he later said of that night, "I never felt so alone."[6] His mother, his brother, and now his father were gone; at the age of twenty, he felt all alone in the world.

But in part as a result of these sufferings, a new life was beginning to call to him. Throughout his twenty years, various teachers and friends suggested that he might be meant for the priesthood, but until that point, he had never taken the idea seriously. Now he began to see the events of his life as leading him irrevocably in that direction and Karol Wojtyla began to form an idea that would exist at the very center of his life for all the decades ahead. It was that God's hand was always at work, and there was no such thing as coincidence, certainly not in his own life. Every incident, every person he had met, every talent he had been given were helping him along the path God had planned for him.

It must be said that to become a priest in Poland at that time required an extra measure of commitment. Indeed, it was nothing less than a life-or-death decision. The seminary that Karol would now begin attending had to be kept secret from the Nazi occupiers. Anyone rumored to be involved with it—much less attending it—could be sent to a concentration camp or put to death by firing squad.

Between keeping up with his work at the chemical factory and his theatrical involvement, Karol also found time to study and attend secret lectures, for the teachers in this underground seminary did not dare to hold actual classes. In charge of Karol's training was Archbishop Sapieha, the man who had seen his potential as a priest several years before.

Despite the careful precautions taken by the seminarians, Karol's life was twice endangered before the end of the war. One incident occurred purely by accident: when walking back from work one day in February 1944, he was hit by a speeding German truck and knocked down, hitting his head. Both a passing Polish woman and a German officer stopped to help him, and he was rushed to the hospital. Karol suffered a bad concussion and had to stay in the hospital for a couple of weeks, but he recovered completely (and managed to find and thank the Polish woman who had helped him).

In August of that same year, he faced a very different kind of threat. The Nazi occupiers were simultaneously being driven back by the invading Russians and dealing with Polish uprisings. The Nazi response to any form of local resistance had always been crushing and brutal, and this would be no different. They conducted a typically thorough security sweep through Krakow, rounding up and marching off all the young men and boys they could find, to what fate one can only imagine. As they came nearer and nearer to the basement apartment that Karol was sharing with friends, the young man prostrated himself on the floor in his room and prayed.

The Nazis came closer and closer—and then passed them by. Whether they didn't see the apartment door or simply forgot about it, no one can say, but the young seminary student and his friends were spared.

After this miraculous delivery, Karol and the other six students at the seminary moved to the archbishop's episcopal residence for safety. They would remain there until the final German retreat from the city in 1945.

When the Jagiellonian University was once again able to reopen, Karol became an assistant instructor in theology there while finishing his studies for the priesthood. One class in particular, a moral theological study of the right to life, would have a profound effect on Karol's personal philosophy in the years ahead.

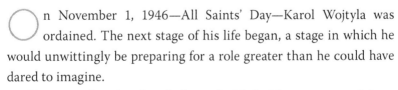

On November 1, 1946—All Saints' Day—Karol Wojtyla was ordained. The next stage of his life began, a stage in which he would unwittingly be preparing for a role greater than he could have dared to imagine.

Yet again, Sapieha played a key role. He had been promoted from archbishop to cardinal early in 1946, and he now sent the young priest to Rome to work toward his doctorate in sacred theology at the Pontifical Angelicum University.

In what was turning out to be a recurring pattern in his life, Karol would have the opportunity to taste several lifestyles at once. At the university, he worked hard on his dissertation about Saint John of the Cross. In his daily life in Rome, he encountered a level of economic prosperity unheard of in Poland, still recovering from the war and also beginning to experience the full force of Soviet tyranny. And on his summer vacation, he traveled to France and Belgium in order to study the new worker-priest movement—a movement that inspired the young student to pronounce: "Catholic intellectual creativity alone will not transform the society."[7]

In Western Europe, Karol for the first time noticed that material wealth often went hand in hand with spiritual poverty. Compared to Poland and those countries behind what would come to be called the Iron Curtain, the Western nations were prosperous, awash in material goods. Yet many of their churches were empty. Well aware of the economic crisis back home and the spiritual crisis surrounding him, he was simultaneously developing his opposition to communism and his critiques of unfettered capitalism.

When he returned to Poland in 1948, Karol became a parish priest, first in a rural parish and then in a more urban one. He continued to teach and to study—he earned a second doctorate, this time in philosophy—and he continued to write plays and poetry but under a pseudonym. He also developed a ministry to youth, marked by his strong empathy and understanding of their needs and struggles. David Aikman writes:

> Karol began conducting hiking trips for young people around the region's mountains and lakes, talking to them in great detail about the challenges they were facing in their lives. Priests were not permitted by the Communists to conduct church meetings outside of their parishes,

so Karol traveled in mufti [civilian dress] with his young charges, men and women, hearing them speak with a frankness unusual in the presence of a priest about sexual temptations and about the struggles of being spiritual in a harshly materialistic and highly controlled society. They talked, joked, and sang deep into the night around campfires, and Karol conducted Mass each morning.

He also took his students to the theater, played chess with them, and had them bring their parents to church-organized functions.[8]

In 1960, at the age of forty, Karol published his first book, *Love and Responsibility*, which had grown out of his work with young adults, especially engaged couples and newlyweds. In it he tackled some of the most contentious issues of the era. The Catholic Church's positions on marriage, sexuality, and family life were under direct assault by the Communist government, and Karol, in his pastoral work, was dealing with the fallout. Poland's Communist government even encouraged young people to have premarital sex, specifically to cause them to break from the church.

Karol argued in his book that sexual love, in order to be all that it was meant to be, must be expressed in the context of responsibility to God and to another person. The sexual ethic of the church, as he framed it, was the way to find true sexual freedom because it helped us learn how to genuinely love others instead of merely using them for our own pleasure. In this book we see an early expression of the sexual ethic he would promote so strongly and consistently during his papacy.

But he expressed that ethic in positive rather than negative terms. Instead of rattling off a list of dos and don'ts, he spoke of a higher good, of real love and real freedom. Weigel points out an often overlooked aspect of Wojtyla's theology here:

Rather than asserting that either the begetting of children or the communion of spouses was the "primary end" of marriage, Wojtyla's sexual ethic taught that love was the norm of marriage, a love in which both the procreative and unitive dimensions of human sexuality reached their full moral value.[9]

His years as a parish priest were among some of the most important and formative years of his life, and crucial to the development of his theology. But eventually he would leave that life behind as his teaching duties increased and he began work on his second doctoral dissertation. It was then that the hardworking priest, educator, and author began to be noticed by influential people within the church hierarchy. In 1958, when he was only thirty-eight, Karol Wojtyla had been named suffragan (subordinate) bishop of Krakow. This appointment was the start of a meteoric rise through the ranks of the Catholic Church—a rise that would bring the largely apolitical priest into unforeseen conflict with Communist government authorities.

To handle this conflict, Wojtyla had to use all his diplomatic skills. He learned to stand up for the church's rights and to promote its presence in Polish society, while at the same time avoiding a direct challenge to the political authorities. His approach helped explain why they regarded him as no significant threat, even as he continued to rise to prominence.

During this period (1962–65), the famous and historic church council that would come to be known as Vatican II was held, and Karol Wojtyla started becoming broadly known in the larger church. Some developments for which he was a strong advocate in that council included the promotion of religious freedom for all, not just for the Catholic Church, and the absolution of the Jewish people as a whole for the Crucifixion of Christ. He argued that "religious freedom . . . touched the heart of the dialogue between the Church and the world, because religious freedom had to do with how the Church thought about the human condition."[10] Though he warned against the potential misuse of freedom, he nonetheless believed it was a crucial and fundamental value, one that the church must consistently advocate for all human beings.

While all this was going on, Wojtyla was made archbishop of Krakow in 1964, and just three years later, Pope Paul VI would make him a cardinal. It was a truly rapid and remarkable rise for a priest who had never involved himself more than he could help with either religious or secular politics (though, when the need arose, he handled it with shrewdness and skill).

A friendship began to grow between him and Pope Paul, who increasingly sought the brilliant and deep-thinking Polish cardinal's advice. Some of Wojtyla's ideas on artificial contraception—namely, his ideas on the dignity and worth of the human person as a creature created and loved by God—would turn up in *Humanae Vitae*, Paul VI's encyclical reiterating the church's opposition to such contraception. Among church leaders, Wojtyla's intellectual vigor and spiritual strength were a powerful and energizing force.

◆ ◆ ◆

As I said in the introduction to this chapter, in August and September of 1978, everything changed. Cardinal Wojtyla's close friend—and the man to whom he had become a confidant and adviser—had died. But who would replace him? There was almost no chance that this Polish cardinal, as close as he had been to Pope Paul, would be elected to the papacy. As a Polish cardinal, he was still something of a second-class citizen in the conclave to elect the next pope. The real power was in the hands of the Italian cardinals, who predictably elected one of their own as Pope John Paul I. Because he was sixty-five, no one dreamed that the new pope was only thirty-three days from death. But very soon after the shortest papacy in history came to its shocking and abrupt close, the cardinals had to convene once more.

David Aikman sets the scene:

> This time, the mood was tense not simply because of the crisis of such a short papal reign, but because there was no longer any consensus on another candidate. The options seemed so wide open that, for the first time, the assembled prelates took the possibility of a foreign pope seriously.[11]

As the conclave went on, the one foreign candidate they began seriously considering was none other than Karol Wojtyla. The diversity of his views attracted a similarly diverse coalition of backers. And it must be that after Pope John Paul I's unexpected demise, the idea of athleticism and youthful vigor forcefully entered the list of things to be considered in a viable candidate.

At last, he was chosen.

During the process, Karol had been seen to turn red and lower his head into his hands. Says George Weigel, "Jerzy Turowicz later wrote that, at the moment of his election, Karol Wojtyla was as alone as a man can be. For to be elected Pope meant 'a clear cut off from one's previous life, with no possible return.'"[12] But when formally asked for his response, he did not hesitate.

"It is God's will," Karol stated. "I accept."

The moment had arrived for the new pope's introduction to the world.

This time, when the name of their new leader was announced, the response of the faithful gathered in Saint Peter's Square was somewhat confused. Usually there is unbridled jubilation. Screams of joy mingle with triumphant shouts of *"Habemus Papam!"* (Latin for "We have a pope!") Flags are waved, and hats soar into the sky. But on this day, the two hundred thousand persons who had gathered—again—were more baffled than anything else. Was it because what was usually a rare occurrence had just happened some weeks before? Or was it simply because no one had ever heard of Karol Wojtyla? Who was this man? And could it really be true that he wasn't Italian?

Part of the reason for the confusion among the faithful that day was that Karol Wojtyla was mostly unknown beyond the leadership of the church itself. Those leaders deeply respected him for his tremendous intellectual and pastoral gifts, but in the wider world he was quite unheard of. Of course all that was about to change in dramatic fashion. But for the moment, it was a fact.

The mood of the crowd began to change as the new pope addressed them directly. This was contrary to precedent, but in the years ahead, he would do much that was contrary to precedent. He now spoke with both humility and contagious confidence. And though a Pole himself, he even spoke in Italian. With a smile, he began, "Jesus Christ be praised!" and then went on:

> Dear brothers and sisters, we are still grieved after the death of our most beloved John Paul I. And now the most eminent cardinals have called a new bishop of Rome from a far-off land; far yet so near through the communion of faith and in the Christian tradition.

He paused at one point to note: "I don't know if I express myself in your—our—Italian language well enough. If I make a mistake, you will correct me."[13]

His openness, vulnerability, and humor drew laughter and applause from the crowd. By the time the extemporaneous speech drew to a close, a remarkable thing had happened: the crowd that was surprised and confused before was now wholeheartedly on John Paul II's side. The observers in Saint Peter's Square—and observers around the world—were with him.

Part of the greatness of this man was his extraordinary ability to communicate humbly and humorously and clearly. There can be no other word for it: he was charming. Like a great politician, but without a hint of guile, he managed to connect with his audiences in a way that delighted them. He would do it many times in the years ahead, but that day in Saint Peter's Square was the first time he did it. And after he had delivered this inaugural speech, he did something else that politicians do, but that popes did not: he waded into the crowd. Aikman writes:

> Wielding his crosier over the crowds in the sign of blessing as though it were a two-edged sword, he kissed babies, embraced worshipers in wheelchairs, and acted as though he had prepared all his life for

a starring role in one of the greatest historical dramas of the twentieth century.[14]

It was a tremendously promising beginning. But who could ever continue along these lines? Yet, a promising beginning was not enough. He must continue as he had begun. At the papal coronation a few days later, he gave every sign of doing just that. His inspiring words rang out above the crowd:

> Be not afraid to welcome Christ and accept his power. Help the Pope and all those who wish to serve Christ and with Christ's power to serve the human person and the whole of mankind.
>
> Be not afraid. Open wide the doors for Christ. To his saving power open the boundaries of states, economic and political systems, the vast fields of culture, civilization, and development.
>
> Be not afraid. Christ knows "what is in man." He alone knows it.[15]

The words of the new pope reflected a lifetime of devotion, trust, humility, and service—the qualities that had equipped him to be one of the greatest leaders of the twentieth century.

But if the man was extraordinary, so, too, were the times in which he was appointed to serve and the tremendously difficult task set for him. Ever since the Second Vatican Council, held in the previous decade, the Catholic Church had been in a state of transition. Wojtyla, then the archbishop of Krakow, participated in that council, designed in large part to help the church adapt to the needs and requirements of the modern world, and he advocated many of its reforms. It was largely because of this that many tended to think of him as a progressive church leader rather than a traditionalist.

People would often make that mistake about the man who became Pope John Paul II. His willingness to embrace change where he believed it was needed and to work across party lines, along with his disarming personality, misled many to think that his inner convictions might be as flexible as his outward manner. Those who believed this were soon disillusioned.

The interesting twist was that even from the disillusioned ones who would have preferred a more progressive pope, John Paul II commanded a mysterious, almost unwilling respect. This was perhaps due to the varied experiences of his life that combined to produce a man who was simultaneously broad-minded in his views and strict in his orthodoxy. But how could this be? A generous broad-mindedness and a serious theological orthodoxy were not two characteristics that one often saw together. It was a baffling blend that both attracted and repelled many observers.

David Aikman quotes one reporter and "liberal Catholic," Jennifer Bradley, as typical of many who weren't quite sure what to make of this man. Writing in the *New Republic*, she said that she was initially "unexcited about the pope," but after attending an outdoor mass celebrated by him in 1995, her perceptions changed: "Now my skepticism will have to share space with awe and, oddly, gratitude."[16]

They felt it as an inherent contradiction, not realizing that John Paul II's views as a whole, including the ones they approved and the ones they disliked, came from the same source: the pope's fervent, long-held belief that we are created in God's image, that we are his beloved children, and that all of our rights, freedoms, and responsibilities come to us from him. That underlying belief drove everything from his stand on sexuality, contraception, and abortion, to his ongoing fight against communism. It was all there, in the writings and teachings of his lifetime, and yet for some reason few of his ideological opponents seemed to figure it out, or fully comprehend it if they did.

◆ ◆ ◆

As he settled into his new role, John Paul II's focus continued to be where it had always been: with, in Jesus' words, "the least of these," the weak and the needy. "When he went out into crowds," according to Levi and Allison, "he was a security nightmare, shaking hands, blessing babies, embracing the elderly and infirm. If he wanted to visit a friend, he just did."[17] At his installation as pope, he made sure that space was reserved in the front row to allow the sick to attend and participate.

The pope also reached out to people of other traditions and faiths, especially Protestants and Jews, in an attempt to reconcile age-old differences and disputes wherever possible. Among Christians, his desire was to further the cause of ecumenism, as he firmly believed that it was God's will; among Jews, he wanted to help heal wounds that had been caused by the church. Wherever he thought it necessary—and this included areas ranging from the Inquisition to the Holocaust—he offered apologies for the church's past conduct.

One emphatic testimony to the effect of what the pope was doing came from the writer and Holocaust survivor Elie Wiesel. After the pope visited the Wailing Wall and put his request for Jewish forgiveness into a chink in the wall, Wiesel told a newspaper, "When I was a child, I was always afraid of walking by a church. Now all of that has changed."[18]

As always, the pope continued to reach out to young people, and they responded with enthusiasm and affection—drawn by his gentle good humor, his openness, his compassion, and above all his unwavering faith.

Levi and Allison note,

> John Paul II's papacy would continue just as it began: as a surprise. He would surprise the papal staff, who frankly could not keep up with him. He would surprise liberals by tightening discipline on the clergy of the Church. He would surprise conservatives with his heartfelt pacifism and ecumenism. He would surprise the Romans by being a more hands-on bishop than any Italian in recent memory.[19]

On May 13, 1981, another surprise was in store. As the pope was entering Saint Peter's Square in Rome, a Turkish assassin named Mehmet Ali Agca pulled out a 9mm semiautomatic pistol and shot the sixty-one-year-old pontiff four times, twice in the abdomen. The pope lost nearly three-quarters of his blood and came near death. But somehow he survived, spending weeks in the hospital recovering. This brush with death brought his priorities into even sharper focus. His friend Cardinal Stanislaw Dziwisz recalls, "He thanked God not only for saving his life but also for allowing him to join the community of the sick who were suffering in the hospital."[20] It was a strange thing to be thankful for, unless one took seriously the words of the Bible about giving thanks in all circumstances, and took seriously the idea of identifying with the weak as Christ had. But of course he did.

So it had always been throughout his life. This man seemed to know the true secret of greatness. He had not sought greatness and had not sought power, but both had come to him as he focused his attention and energy, as Christ taught, on those who were least able to reciprocate. As pope, he did not always accomplish what he set out to accomplish, but there were times when his mere presence seemed to inspire change. For instance, reflecting on one aspect of the pope's opposition to communism and its effect on his native country, David Aikman notes:

> Some have denied any connection between the sense of exultation created in Poles by John Paul's visit in June 1979 and the sudden emergence of the Solidarity free trade union in Gdansk in August of the following year. Certainly there would have been labor troubles in Poland no matter who had been pope at the time. But would the results have been anything like what they turned out to be if John Paul had not carefully nurtured the events in his own country throughout the 1980's decade? It doesn't seem likely.[21]

Again, without adopting a confrontational style, the man whom Polish Communist authorities had once regarded as relatively harmless became one of the key figures in the collapse of communism across Europe. Though he clashed at times with US leaders over the use of military force, which he deplored, in his own way he worked in tandem with them to defeat the Soviet regime, standing up for human rights and giving aid and comfort to foes of communism, such as Solidarity leader Lech Walesa, even as he avoided direct conflict with Communist leaders.

In his demanding and multifaceted role, the pope's relative youth and his exuberant health sustained him for a long time. Stories were told of unsuspecting skiers who were surprised to catch sight of the head of the Catholic Church enjoying himself on the slopes. But as the twentieth century drew to a close, his health slowly started to fail. He began to show clear symptoms of Parkinson's disease.

And so Pope John Paul II began to live out the last great paradox of his life: in suffering and weakness, he would show God's strength. As a man once known for his athleticism and vigor, he was uncomfortable appearing in public when his health was obviously failing. But that failure, many believed, helped him identify more strongly with the sufferings of Christ on the cross and, by extension, with the sufferings of people everywhere.

He also used his disease to call attention to the need for a cure for Parkinson's and to publicly draw the distinction, as so few were willing to draw it at that time, between ethical and unethical methods of research. In accordance with his beliefs about the sacredness of all human life, the pope took an unyielding stand against the use of human embryonic stem cells in medical research.

The press seldom acknowledged the remarkable courage and selflessness of his stand. Many members of the US mainstream media, for instance, fervently supported embryonic stem cell research and were far more apt to make heroes of those with Parkinson's and other disabilities, such as Michael J. Fox and Christopher Reeve, who fought to advance it. Ironically, in doing so, the media missed a truly heroic story of the man who took a firm stand against what appeared, at the time, to be in his own self-interest. (As it happens, later developments in the research brought into question the effectiveness of treatment with embryonic stem cells. But just a few years ago, the popular narrative was more or less that the use of these cells would be the cure to end all cures.)

One typical article, on CNN's website, reported on John Paul's meeting with George W. Bush, in which the pope strongly urged the president not to fund such research. The article covered the Vatican's uncompromising stand on the issue, the president's dilemma, and various other related issues. And then, in the very last paragraph:

> Scientists believe research using stem cells might unlock cures for diseases including Alzheimer's, Parkinson's and diabetes, as well as spinal cord injuries. The pope himself suffers from symptoms of Parkinson's disease.[22]

It would be hard to surpass that for understatement.

Once again, the pope was identifying with some of the weakest and most helpless members of society: in this case the unborn. And though it received scant notice, no statement on their behalf could have been more powerful than his unwillingness to sacrifice these helpless ones to benefit himself.

One of the most memorable images of Pope John Paul II from these last years of his life—perhaps one of the most memorable images ever taken of him at all—was taken in 2005 during the *Via Crucis*, the Good Friday marking of the Stations of the Cross. For the first time that year, John Paul II was too ill to lead the walk. But as George Weigel observes in his book *The End and the Beginning: Pope John Paul II—The Victory of Freedom, the Last Years, the Legacy*, in effect he still did lead it, albeit in a different way:

> As Cardinal Ratzinger led the solemn procession through the ruins of antiquity, John Paul II prayed the *Via Crucis* while watching the ceremony at the Colosseum on a television set that had been placed

in the chapel of the papal apartment. A television camera at the door of the chapel showed the world John Paul's prayer. He was seated, and grasped in his arms a large crucifix, as he prayed through the fourteen stations with the congregation near the Roman Forum. Those watching at the Colosseum and on television could see only John Paul's back; his face was never shown. Contrary to press speculations, however, he was not hiding his pain or the ravages of weeks of illness. Rather, he was doing what he had always done, which was not to say, "Look at me," but rather, "Look to Christ."[23]

Whereas once he was known as a physically vigorous and strong man, he was now seen as a man who was forced to rely more fully than ever on Christ for all things, in the physical as well as in the spiritual realm. And he was loved all the more for it.

He would not live much longer; less than a week after that vigil in the chapel, he developed septic shock following a urinary tract infection. Deathly ill, he tried to bless the Easter crowd in Saint Peter's Square but was unable to speak and could only make the sign of the cross over them three times before withdrawing. On April 2, as he lay dying, he conveyed to those around him that he had a message for the young people gathered outside his window, still faithful to the leader they loved: "I have sought you out. Now you have come to me. I thank you."[24] A few hours later, he was gone.

As Dr. Jean Bethke Elshtain of the University of Chicago recalled at one of our Socrates in the City events in New York City (the transcript is available in *Socrates in the City: Conversations on "Life, God, and Other Small Topics"*), the pope's funeral produced "an outpouring of humanity that took the media utterly by surprise." She added:

> By then, it shouldn't have taken them by surprise, because it happened every time he did anything. But what struck me were the millions of young people who turned up and stayed there under these very difficult conditions for days, in order that they could be present.

Something was calling to them. He somehow spoke to them, even in his infirm old age, with the Parkinson's and all the rest. If we could think this through with you—it would be a very interesting exercise considering what that embodied and what hope that represented—we could see some possible sparks for a certain kind of renewal of our humanity more fully understood.

Such a renewal was indeed the legacy of Pope John Paul II. In his strengths and weaknesses alike, he demonstrated charity and compassion born out of his belief that every human being is a beloved child of God. George Weigel, a Catholic, acknowledges that Pope John Paul II at times made serious errors in judgment, but that even these were usually connected to his "profound disinclination to humiliate, or make a spectacle of, someone else; his intense dislike of gossip; his occasional tendency to project his own virtues onto others; and his determination to find something good in another's actions or words."[25] But the strength of his beliefs, Weigel adds, was that they sustained him in "radical self-giving . . . only possible through the grace of God in Christ."[26]

From a Protestant point of view, David Aikman quotes Billy Graham's statement that Pope John Paul II was "the strong conscience of the whole Christian world," and then Aikman reflects:

I am not a Roman Catholic, and I certainly share many of the Protestant reservations about some aspects of Catholic doctrine and some forms of Catholic devotionalism. Yet it is my view that Pope John Paul II, in his profound spiritual depth, his prayer life, his enormous intellectual universe, his compassion and sympathy for the oppressed, and above all in his vision of how Christians collectively are supposed to live, is the greatest single Christian leader of the twentieth century.[27]

There is much to be said for that view. Through the paradoxes of his life—achieving strength through weakness, power through humility, generosity and broad-mindedness through orthodoxy—Pope John Paul II exemplified Christ's radical and revolutionary teaching that whoever loses his life shall find it. In his judicious exercise of power and his identification with the powerless, he was a Christian leader of a theological and moral stature that we have seldom seen in our lifetimes.

SEVEN

Charles W. Colson

1931–2012

His memorial service took place at Washington National Cathedral on a beautiful spring day, May 16, 2012. Familiar faces were everywhere.

Journalists Brit Hume, Fred Barnes, and Cal Thomas were there. So were human-rights advocates Michael Horowitz, Joni Eareckson Tada, and former congressman Jim Ryun, who in 1964 had been the first high schooler to break the four-minute mile. I also saw the writer Joe Loconte. The gifted gospel singer Wintley Phipps was there, too, and sang "Amazing Grace."

President Reagan's attorney general, Ed Meese, was there. President Clinton's special counsel, Lanny Davis, was there. President George W. Bush's chief speechwriter, Michael Gerson, was there.

They were all present to honor the man who had worked hard, in his younger years, for President Richard Nixon—the most powerful man on earth, but who spent the second half of his life working even harder for the King of kings.

I was there to honor a man I loved, whose life had been a powerful inspiration to me, and whom I had been privileged to know and work for and call a friend.

I would have been astonished had I known, as a ten-year-old reading the newspapers in 1973, that I would one day befriend the notorious Watergate hatchet man, Charles W. Colson. He was one of that crew—H. R. Haldeman, John Erlichman, and G. Gordon Liddy—whose disregard for truth in their blind service of power brought a great nation to the edge of ruin.

After I came to faith in 1988, I heard Chuck Colson's name again, this time identifying him as the founder of Prison Fellowship Ministries. Not long afterward, a friend turned me on to his books.

Those books! Reading them was a revelation. First, I read his auto-biography, *Born Again*, and then I read *Loving God* and *Kingdoms in Conflict*. They were a tremendous education for someone hungry to learn about his new faith.

A few years later I heard that Chuck was speaking at Yale Law School in New Haven, and I practically raced there to hear him. I even wrote a long letter to him, introducing myself and gushing about how much his work had meant to me, and I placed it inside a children's book I had written *(Uncle Mugsy and the Terrible Twins of Christmas)*, which I inscribed to his grandchildren. When he came off the stage, I shook his hand and handed him the book and letter. Not much more than a week later, I got a letter in return. I was stag-gered. The letter said something about how much my letter meant to him, and it added that he would keep it in his files, that per-haps we might work together someday. I almost couldn't believe my eyes, but I chalked it up as probably a well-meaning but unrealistic sentiment.

Of course, I didn't know Chuck Colson very well at that point, but about a year later I got a phone call from his office. The caller said they were in need of a writer and editor for *BreakPoint*, the daily radio com-mentary that Chuck had been doing for a few years. Was I interested in applying for the job? I was amazed that Chuck, who probably wrote thousands of letters every year, remembered our correspondence. But I applied and got the job, and suddenly I was working with my hero, Chuck Colson. Working for Chuck was deeply gratifying, but it was tough too; he may have been a redeemed marine, but he was still a marine. After two years I was exhausted enough to decide to take a different kind of job, working for VeggieTales. Bob the Tomato was a much less demanding boss and had never been in the marines. But Chuck and I kept in touch.

A few years later I was able to get Chuck to agree to speak at a forum I founded in New York City called Socrates in the City. He spoke for us twice. The first time was at the Union League Club in Manhattan in 2006. The room was packed with 350 people, and when Chuck finished, the audience exploded into powerful applause. As the applause continued, Chuck walked down the center aisle triumphantly, shaking hands left and right. Everyone there said that it was as though he had just given the State of the Union address.

The second time Chuck came to speak at Socrates in the City was in December 2010 for our Christmas gala. Again, it was a tremendous event.

I was there the day Chuck fell ill during his final speaking engagement in Virginia on March 30, 2012. In fact, I introduced him for what would become his last speech. Toward the end of it, he couldn't continue, and a doctor was summoned. As he was lying on a gurney, waiting to be put into the ambulance, I put my arm on his shoulder and just stood there, wanting him to feel the comfort of a human touch. Then I said, half-joking, not knowing if he was able to take it in: "Is there anything you want me to tell the crowd, Chuck?"

But he did get it. "Just tell them that I'm so sorry to have ruined everyone's evening!" And those were the last words I would ever hear from this great man and friend. How I miss him. But I take real comfort in knowing that I'll see him again.

Like all the stories in this book, it's the story of an inspiring and a great man. May it inspire you to greatness.

◆ ◆ ◆

C harles Wendell Colson was first born during the Great Depression, on October 16, 1931, in North Boston to Inez "Dizzy" and Wendell Colson. I say "first born" because Chuck would be born again many years later, but let's not get ahead of ourselves. Chuck's father worked as a bookkeeper at a meatpacking plant, and eventually, by attending night school, he earned a law degree.

Chuck was one of those children born with extraordinary gifts of drive and intelligence. In his book *The Good Life*, Chuck tells the story of how as an eleven-year-old boy during World War II, he led a successful drive to raise money for a jeep for the American armed forces.

But Chuck's parents were ambitious, too, and they made many sacrifices so their only child could attend the prestigious Browne and Nichols School in Cambridge, Massachusetts. It was one of those schools whose *raison d'etre* seemed to be getting its students into the Ivy League. In Chuck's case, it succeeded. In fact Chuck was offered two full college scholarships: one to Harvard and another, a Navy ROTC scholarship, to Brown. In what happened next, we see an early instance of Chuck's pride revealing itself.

"As a boy I used to stand on the pebbly beach looking across the gray-green waters of the harbor at the city then run by the Brahmins, the Beacon Hill establishment which traced its ancestry through generations of Harvard classes back to the *Mayflower*," Chuck recalled.

> We were neither the new ethnics—Italians, Irish Catholics just seizing political power in the wards of Boston—nor old stock. "Swamp Yankees," we were called. Acceptance was what we were denied— and what we most fervently sought. Now in this one moment, I had it—admission to the elite. And in my pride I believed I had something better still—the chance to turn them down.[1]

Chuck turned down Harvard, choosing to attend Brown instead. He graduated with honors in 1953, and not long afterward, he married

Nancy Billings of Boston. In the next few years the couple became the parents of three children: two boys—Wendell and Christian—and a daughter named Emily.

In the same year that he graduated and got married, Chuck received his commission in the Marine Corps, serving in Korea just after the end of major US involvement there. With his typical drive and ambition, Chuck rose quickly in the marine's ranks to become the youngest captain in their long and fabled history. It was during his time with the marines that Chuck, who had been raised in the Episcopal Church, had his first serious thoughts about God.

During the summer of 1954, Chuck and his battalion were sent to the coast of Guatemala, where Communists were engaged in an uprising. The US Marines had been summoned to protect the lives of the Americans living there.

Standing on the deck of the USS *Mellette* on a hot, dark night, Chuck—a bit fearful of what might happen in the days ahead—looked up at the millions of stars sparkling in the inky sky. "That night I suddenly became as certain as I had ever been about anything in my life that out there in that great starlit beyond was God," Chuck writes in *Born Again.* "I was convinced that He ruled over the universe, that to Him there were no mysteries, that He somehow kept it all miraculously in order. In my own fumbling way, I prayed, knowing that He was there, questioning only whether He had time to hear me."[2]

Guatemala's pro-US regime dealt with the Communists on its own, and not long afterward, Chuck resigned his commission and entered George Washington University Law School, taking classes at night and working during the day. He graduated—again with honors—in 1959. Throughout the 1950s, Chuck also had become involved in politics. In fact back in 1948, when he was just seventeen, he had volunteered with the campaign of Massachusetts governor Robert F. Bradford, and there he learned his first lessons in campaign dirty tricks, from planting fake news stories to spying on the opposition. So now, when he was called upon to manage the 1960 reelection campaign of Massachusetts senator Leverett Saltonstall, he would employ all the dirty tricks he had learned in 1948, and invented a few of his own. Saltonstall won.

Following this victory, Chuck and his friend Charlie Morin opened their own law firm, which became highly successful. His personal life was far less so. Chuck writes that his obsession with politics, which his wife did not share, was driving them apart. The couple eventually divorced, and in 1964, Chuck married the woman who would be his wife for the next forty-eight years: Patty Hughes.

◆ ◆ ◆

Chuck's unprincipled rise to giddy heights of power and his spectacular fall from those heights are the proverbial stuff of legend. Despite the career-induced failure of his marriage, Chuck's drive to the top continued, unabated and without course correction.

He became involved in the 1968 presidential campaign, working hard to elect Richard Nixon. The long hours and hard work paid off: Nixon won. But they would pay off in an even greater way: in 1969 Nixon appointed Chuck to be his special counsel. For Chuck Colson, it was the ultimate prize. At age thirty-eight, he had the ear and the confidence of the most powerful human being on the planet.

Chuck's gung-ho nature, coupled with his brilliance and a strong desire to please the president, quickly made him Nixon's go-to guy in every situation. He would do virtually anything for the president, and before long Nixon was egging him on to cut corners and make things happen, no matter the cost.

Those who knew him at the time saw that a certain ruthlessness had overtaken Chuck. In his own mind, of course, it was all for a good cause. He viewed his actions in comparison to the actions of others; so it was always the other guy who started the fight. It was always the other guy who had behaved ruthlessly first. What else could he do, Chuck reasoned, but return fire?

Of course this sort of moral reasoning—or lack of moral reasoning—will soon lead anyone into a swamp of self-deceit. In the case of

Chuck Colson and many others in the Nixon administration, that self-deceit led to the historic political meltdown known as Watergate.

Watergate was such a game-changing scandal in the history of American politics that almost every political scandal since has had the *-gate* suffix attached to it. And although it all hinged on a ridiculous burglary in the Watergate Hotel, it was part of something much bigger. That burglary was just the symptom of the ugly atmosphere that had taken over the Nixon White House, and Chuck Colson was at the center of it.

In the fall of 1972, Nixon was reelected in a landslide, in some large part due to Chuck's brilliant—and sometimes underhanded—political maneuverings. But in the dark, pragmatic, and ungrateful world of the Nixon White House, such values as loyalty didn't count for much. As the Watergate scandal mushroomed, it became evident to Nixon and his aides Haldeman and Erlichman that Chuck, despite all he had done, was a political liability. So they decided to make him a scapegoat. Not long after the November victory, the president made it clear that Chuck had to go. Chuck wasn't happy, but in the rough-and-tumble world of politics, this sort of thing happened. There was nothing he could do.

And so, taking up his post-White House life, Chuck began to rebuild his law practice. One of the biggest clients he hoped to land was that of the Raytheon Company, located in Massachusetts. In mid-March 1973, Chuck found himself in the offices of Tom Phillips, Raytheon's CEO.

But something had happened to the successful titan of industry in the previous week: Phillips had accepted Christ at a Billy Graham Crusade. At the end of his meeting with Chuck, Phillips said, "I'd like to tell you the whole story someday of how I came to Christ. I had gotten to the point where I didn't think my life was worth anything. Now I have committed my life to him, everything has changed—attitude, values, the whole bit. If you'd like to hear more, give me a call."[3]

Chuck was uncomfortable with such talk and didn't intend to

continue the conversation. But Phillips had a feeling that Chuck was more interested than he realized and waited to hear from him.

Meanwhile, the Watergate scandal was growing. On July 16, 1973, a bombshell exploded when a lower-level White House aide revealed that Nixon had secretly taped most of his Oval Office conversations. This news reinvigorated those who were out to get Nixon, and in the hue and cry that followed, Chuck cringed to think about some of the things he had said in the false privacy of the Oval Office—words that were almost certainly on those tapes.

News reporters and cameras were now stationed outside Chuck's home, and three times the FBI was called to investigate bomb threats. It was madness. Chuck escaped the gathering storm by taking a trip that August to the Maine seacoast, stopping en route to visit his parents in Massachusetts. While he was there, he decided to visit Tom Phillips at his home in Weston wanting to know more about why Phillips had considered his life empty despite having achieved such success in business. The brewing troubles of Watergate were bringing about a newfound introspection in Chuck, so that now, if only to himself, he grudgingly began to acknowledge that he, too, felt an emptiness inside, despite all his remarkable achievements.

At Phillips's home, Chuck asked what had happened to alter him so dramatically.

"I would go to the office each day and do my job," Phillips recalled, "striving all the time to make the company succeed, but there was a big hole in my life. I began to read the scriptures, looking for answers. Something made me realize I needed a personal relationship with God."[4]

Chuck was skeptical of the whole thing. It all sounded too simple and to some extent ridiculous.

But as the conversation turned back to Watergate, and Chuck began trying to justify his actions in the whole mess—pointing the blame at Nixon's enemies—Phillips pushed back. He saw it was pride that had led Chuck and the other Nixonites to do what they did. He pulled out a paperback copy of C. S. Lewis's famous book *Mere Christianity*, and there on the screened porch, he read aloud from chapter 8, "The Great Sin: Pride."

As Phillips read about how pride corrupts us, Chuck cringed, but not because he was embarrassed. It was because he began to recognize himself in the description. He knew that Lewis's words applied to him in particular. It was indeed his own pride that had corrupted him, twisted his thinking, and led to the frightening circumstances in which he now found himself. As Chuck recalled some of the prideful ways he had behaved over the course of his life, and most recently as Nixon's special counsel, he felt an agony of shame.

Yet when Phillips stopped reading and asked Chuck for his response to what he'd heard, Chuck made it clear that he wasn't ready to accept Christ into his life; the deep skepticism toward religious conversion remained. Phillips pressed ahead, reading aloud from Psalm 37. "Do not fret," it said. "Trust in the LORD and do good. . . . Delight yourself in the LORD and he will give you the desires of your heart. Commit your way to the LORD; trust in him and he will do this."[5] It all sounded powerfully inviting to Chuck in his hour of need.

Then Phillips read the third chapter of John's gospel, where Jesus tells Nicodemus that he must be born again. He then asked Chuck if he could pray for him. Chuck was not expecting this question and hardly knew what to say, but he was in enough turmoil that he wasn't about to refuse. He allowed Phillips to proceed.

"As Tom prayed, something began to flow into me—a kind of energy," Chuck recalls in *Born Again*. "Then came a wave of emotion which nearly brought tears. I fought them back. It sounded as if Tom were speaking directly and personally to God, almost as if he were sitting beside us."[6]

Phillips gave Chuck his copy of *Mere Christianity* and some other reading material and said that a friend of his named Doug Coe might be in touch with him to continue the conversation. That was it. Chuck bade his friend good-bye and walked out into the August night.

Then the floodgates opened. Sitting alone in his car, Chuck, the marine, take-no-prisoners tough guy, began to sob. Filled with emotion, he realized that he should go back into Phillips's house and pray with his friend. But now when he glanced at the house, he saw the lights being switched off. It was too late.

Chuck drove toward home, but he realized that he was weeping so copiously he could scarcely see the road. Afraid he might crash into an oncoming car, he pulled over. And there, alone in the night, by the side of a road, Chuck Colson gave his heart to God.

"God, I don't know how to find you," he prayed, "but I'm going to try! I'm not much the way I am now, but somehow I want to give myself over to you."[7]

Over and over as he sat there in the car, Chuck asked God to receive him. It was a humble prayer by a man the world knew as anything but humble. As Chuck relates in *Born Again*,

> I had not "accepted" Christ—I still didn't know who He was. My mind told me it was important to find that out first, to be sure that I knew what I was doing. . . . Only that night something inside me was urging me to surrender—to what or to whom I did not know. I stayed there in the car, wet-eyed, praying, thinking for perhaps half an hour, perhaps longer, alone in the dark of the quiet night. Yet for the first time in my life I was not alone at all.[8]

How many drivers in cars passing on that strip of roadway that evening wondered why that car was parked there on the side of the road? Who could have guessed that inside it there was a famous man, a national figure, weeping and humbling himself before the God of the universe? Little did they know that a holy transaction was taking place, one that would affect the lives of millions in the decades to come.

Chuck told no one about what happened that night except Patty. His wife had been a churchgoing Catholic for her entire life, but she wasn't conversant in the terminology of evangelical Christianity. So when Chuck asked her if she knew what a conversion experience was, her answer was a short no.

Chuck told her that he had experienced one. Patty might not have known what a conversion experience was, but she could tell that whatever happened to her husband, it was good.

As with all true mysteries, the mystery of conversion cannot be dissected very effectively. Does conversion take place in a single moment? Or is it a process? What happens in such a conversion? In the case of Chuck Colson, as with William Wilberforce and so many others, there was no way to say. All Chuck knew was that at one moment he had asked God into his heart in a simple way and that the desire to do so had come out of his brokenness. After it happened, he had a strong desire to learn more. He said yes to something with his whole being, but he still had a strong desire to find out just what he said yes to.

In the following week, as he and Patty enjoyed their time on the Maine coast, Chuck went to work. He had brought along *Mere Christianity* and a raft of yellow legal pads. In his sometimes comically thorough and deliberate way, Chuck made notes and followed the arguments like the brilliant lawyer that he was. He wasn't about to accept something without thinking it through.

At first, the idea that he had to accept not just God, but Jesus, was confusing. How could he logically accept a two-thousand-year-old historical figure from Palestine as the God of the universe? It seemed absurd. Then he read the famous passage in Lewis's book where Lewis lays out the three alternatives in no uncertain terms, saying that Jesus was either Lord, liar, or lunatic. The alternative not open to us is to think of Jesus merely as a powerful moral teacher. It was clear and it was discomfiting. Chuck knew that in his encounter with the mind of C. S. Lewis, he had met his match. The man's logic was irrefutable.

"There was my choice as simple, stark and frightening as that," Chuck later recalled. "No fine shadings, no gradations, no compromises. No one had ever thrust this truth at me in such a direct and unsettling way."[9]

Chuck was afraid that in his desperate state he might make an illogical leap, so he continued to wrestle with the arguments. But on his sixth day with Patty in that Maine cottage, he knew his mind was made up, and he prayed a simple prayer, asking Jesus to come into his life.

◆ ◆ ◆

Returning to Washington, Chuck resumed the process of building up his post-White House law practice. But Watergate kept intruding. Every day there was some fresh humiliation. The media savaged Chuck, reveling in the downfall of the so-called White House hatchet man who—in their eyes and in the eyes of many others—was finally getting his just deserts.

As a brand-new Christian, Chuck had no idea how his newfound faith related to the hell through which he was now going.

"I was about as stressed out as a guy can possibly be," he recalled.

Every night I would have at least three or four large scotch and sodas in the hope of drowning it all out. I was waking up in the morning as tired as when I had gone to bed the night before. In the middle of the night I was waking up, sometimes to think about prison but more often to get angry about things being said about me that were untrue. . . . My greatest agony in this period was hearing something or seeing something written about me that was completely wrong. So I'd try and correct it by testifying or by writing a letter, only to find out that nobody would believe me. It was excruciating torture.[10]

Besides Patty, Chuck's most consistent solace in the midst of this unending storm was a small group of men who had invited him into their circle of Christian fellowship in Washington, DC. They were part of the Fellowship, a fiercely bipartisan group of Christians who met regularly for prayer. The leader of this group was Doug Coe, who had begun the National Prayer Breakfast during the Eisenhower administration. Once Coe learned from Tom Phillips that Chuck had turned his life over to God, he invited himself into Chuck's life and dragged him into the group of men who eventually became his closest friends.

One of them was the ferociously liberal Iowa senator Harold Hughes. Hughes was one of the most well-known enemies of the Nixon White House, and Chuck couldn't believe that such a man would have anything to do with him. But once Chuck told Hughes that he had accepted Jesus, Hughes embraced him in a bear hug and told him that all was forgiven. "I love you now as my brother in Christ. I will stand with you, defend you anywhere, and trust you with anything I have," Hughes promised.[11]

Chuck had never experienced anything like this. Could it be for real? He was quickly amazed to learn that it was. Hughes and the other men of the Fellowship became his closest allies during the painful months to come. They went far out of their way to emphasize bipartisanship, teaching Chuck that a relationship with Jesus should never be used as a political tool. Chuck knew that his newfound faith would baffle as many on the political right, who had been his allies, as on the left, who hated him.

This understanding established in Chuck a desire to remain above the political fray whenever possible. The four-decades-long advocacy for prisoners that would become his life's chief legacy would be the principal example of this view.

As the months passed, the pressures of the metastasizing Watergate scandal were getting worse. Chuck's aggressive, no-holds-barred public defense of Nixon in the past year would now bite back. After Nixon himself, Special Prosecutor Leon Jaworski most wanted Colson. Viciousness and ruthlessness had characterized the way Chuck had dealt with his political enemies, and it would now characterize how Jaworski dealt with him. He was reaping what he had sown.

Chuck was in a terrible spot, and he knew it. The fear of going to prison was very real for him. He had heard about the grotesque reality of prison rape, and he knew that there was a very palpable possibility of other kinds of violence against him. It was an indisputable fact that some prisoners, convinced that their lives were hell because of government officials, would have liked nothing better than to get revenge on a high-profile White House figure like Chuck Colson.

Realizing that he could put the screws to Colson, Jaworski offered him a plea bargain, asking Chuck to plead guilty to the misdemeanor charge of conspiring to break into the offices of Daniel Ellsberg's psychiatrist. Chuck had engaged in many dirty tricks, but this simply was not one of them. Yet to save his own skin and be allowed to continue to practice as a lawyer and feed his family, he would have to lie. It would have been a prudent thing to do, and Chuck's lawyer made it clear that refusing this deal would be sheer insanity. He must take it and move on with his life.

But as a new Christian, Chuck felt deeply uncomfortable with the thought of lying, even to save his own skin. He was no longer a man of mere pragmatism. He believed he had to honor God with everything he said and did, to the best of his abilities. Stating that he had done something he had not actually done seemed wrong.

What did his family think? Chuck consulted with them, and their response bolstered him in his decision. It was settled. Chuck then gave the hard news to his lawyer, who exploded with fury. But Chuck felt confident that if he honored God in this matter, God would honor him.

Chuck soon discovered that God doesn't always honor us in the way we think he should. Chuck refused the deal, and the prosecutors promptly indicted him on felony charges.

Thus the media circus surrounding the Watergate scandal continued, with new revelations emerging almost daily. A group of Nixon's secret tapes were then released to the public. Could it get any worse? They painted a picture of deviousness, lying, and just plain nastiness inside the White House, and it was painful for Chuck to realize he had been part of it all.

Chuck had been no idle bystander. He knew in his heart that he had contributed to the amoral—and often deeply immoral—atmosphere in the White House. He knew that even if he wasn't guilty of what he was being accused of, he was certainly guilty in other ways. In the eyes of God, which was the only judgment that really counted, he was terribly guilty.

The pugnacious side of Colson was not dead yet, though. It was very much alive and kicking, as twenty million viewers discovered when he made his now famous appearance on CBS's *60 Minutes*. Although Chuck had become a devout Christian, he was also the defendant in an important case, and he had to figure out how to reconcile these two elements. How could he defend himself while knowing his guilt in so many other matters?

During the interview, Chuck saw that he was trying to have things both ways, vigorously defending himself before the court of public opinion while trying to be an outspoken Christian. It wouldn't work. His pugnacious side could not coexist with his new life in Christ.

Chuck decided that the only way to go forward was one that made no sense to anyone except his handful of Christian friends. In fact, it would make refusing the plea bargain seem like child's play. He decided to voluntarily confess to something that he *had* done and trust God with the outcome. He might have to go to prison, but if he did, he knew that God would go with him. To many, the idea sounded insane. Why would anyone do such a thing?

Even Patty was skeptical, but Chuck assured her that this really was the only way forward, the only way that things would get better. Chuck would be putting everything in God's hands. He knew he could trust God with the whole thing and that somehow it would be okay. Of course, Chuck's lawyer did not see it that way. In fact, his reaction to hearing this proposed course of action is unprintable. But Chuck wouldn't back down.

He had decided to plead guilty to "disseminating derogatory information to the press about Daniel Ellsberg while he was a criminal defendant."[12] This was true, and although many didn't think it constituted an actual obstruction of justice, Chuck figured the judge would accept it as such and would probably be inclined to show at least a little mercy.

And so Chuck Colson pled guilty to this act. But Judge Gerhard Gesell didn't show one iota of mercy. He didn't seem to care that Chuck had done this purely voluntarily. He threw the book at him anyway, stunning witnesses by imposing a sentence of one to three years. Patty, who was in the courtroom, was the most horrified of anyone.

After the sentencing, Chuck had to face the media on the courthouse steps. What he said there was not what the assembled members of the Fourth Estate were expecting. It was not what anyone was expecting to hear. In fact, what he said was as staggering as the harsh sentence. "What happened in court today," Chuck said, "was the court's will and the Lord's will. I have committed my life to Jesus Christ and I can work for him in prison as well as out." What Chuck said was quite true, but he didn't know at the time that this extraordinary statement would prove to be prophetic.[13]

Of course the press had a field day with Chuck's conversion. The *Los Angeles Times* published a cartoon by the famous political cartoonist Pat Oliphant featuring Chuck dressed as a medieval monk, painting the word *Repent* on the gates of the White House. Another cartoon showed him walking past a shocked Nixon while carrying a placard that said, "The End Is Nigh."

The media—whose members tend to be more secular than not—could not get their minds around what was happening to Chuck Colson. He was being transformed, but in their world, this sort of thing simply didn't occur. Nasty people like Chuck Colson didn't change overnight and start being kind to others. Chuck had to be making a Machiavellian maneuver, designed to garner sympathy from the prosecutor or at least from the world of public opinion.

Just as the apostle Paul had once been a zealous persecutor of Christians and had been literally blinded by the Light and transformed into the most zealous Christian of them all, Chuck Colson really was a changed man. But some observers could not accept it, and some would never accept it. Even at the end of his life—after nearly forty years of serving God and prisoners in prisons and beyond—some people refused to believe he had ever changed.

◆ ◆ ◆

On July 8, 1974, Chuck entered the US prison system, becoming prisoner number 23226. After a short time at Holabird detention center in Baltimore, he was transferred to Maxwell Federal Prison Camp in Alabama. He endured the typical humiliations and indignities of prison life, trading in his Brooks Brothers suit for an ugly brown uniform and underwear that had been worn by previous prisoners. There were rats and roaches to deal with, as well as racial tension. One day a friendly prisoner told Chuck that he had overheard someone talk about "killing Colson," and he said that it didn't sound like an idle boast.

Chuck was determined to show that he wasn't someone special—or that he didn't think of himself as someone special—so he volunteered for a number of menial chores, such as mopping floors. One day an African American man asked him, "How you like living with the scum after having all those servants in the White House?"[14] But seeing the man was young, Chuck replied that he'd been doing things like this years before the younger man had been born, and that he'd served in the marines while the other man had still been in diapers.

Somehow this seemed to do the trick. Word spread that Colson was okay.

While Chuck worked in the prison laundry, he would leave his Bible out, hoping someone might notice and start a conversation about it. No one did. The prison atmosphere was closed to anything having to do with God.

But now that he was in prison, Chuck was even more interested in learning what the Bible had to say, and he undertook a serious Bible study. One day he read Hebrews 2:11: "For the one who makes men holy and the men who are made holy share a common humanity. So that [Jesus] is not ashamed to call them his brothers" (PHILLIPS).

Something about this passage got to Chuck. In reading those words he suddenly understood why he was in prison. If Jesus, who was God in the flesh, was not ashamed to call human beings his brothers, perhaps the high-and-mighty Chuck Colson, who had had an office next to the president of the United States, was put here to do the same thing—to empty his pride and call his fellow prisoners his brothers and to know that they really were his brothers.

For Chuck, it was nothing less than a divine revelation, an epiphany. He saw that his prison sentence and his suffering were part of a grand and holy scheme. God had humbled him and brought him there precisely so that Chuck could help these men. Chuck now knew that his life had not been destroyed by coming to prison; instead, prison was part of God's greater purposes. It was the beginning of something wonderful and new. With that, everything changed.

Suddenly, Chuck was zealous to make an impact for God right there in the prison. The first thing he would do was try to recreate something of the fellowship he had on the outside with members of the Fellowship. It wouldn't be easy. Even the one prisoner who told Chuck that he had "accepted the Lord" wasn't interested. He was afraid of the abuse he'd have to take if someone saw him getting involved in a Bible study. It just wasn't the thing to do. Better to keep your head down and not draw attention to yourself, he advised.

Then one day Chuck met a passionate Christian named Tex. Chuck overheard him talking about a fellow prisoner named Bob Ferguson, who had five kids and desperately needed the parole board to let him out. The odds were strongly against his being released, but it was such a desperate situation that Tex said they should pray with Ferguson. They needed a real miracle. That's all Chuck needed to hear, and he leaped in, offering to join them. The pair found Ferguson, and both men prayed for him. The small group of inmates who surrounded them were impressed by Chuck's prayer.

And the next day the miracle actually happened. Ferguson got his parole. Almost instantly, four or five men were interested in joining Chuck's prayer and Bible study group.

Chuck now began to help prisoners in other ways too. One inmate who was unable to read or write asked Chuck to help him write a letter to the judge who could grant him parole. Such needs broke his heart. Although he'd been advised not to use his legal expertise to help other inmates, "I could not refuse those who needed help," Chuck said. "These were my brothers. The Lord had shown the way and now I was following."[15]

Over time, Chuck saw that God had brought him to Maxwell not only to teach him that his fellow prisoners were his brothers in Christ but also so that he could identify with them and see the world from their perspective. Only after he had done this would he be able to effectively help them. Chuck didn't know what lay ahead, but he knew that he wanted to fulfill God's purpose for his life, so he continued doing what he was doing. He was confident the Lord would reveal his plan in his own time.

One weekend, Chuck had a visit from an old friend, Fred "Dusty" Rhodes, who had been a committed Christian for many years. The little group Chuck had gathered at Maxwell impressed Dusty, and he was affected by Chuck's vision for prison ministry. Fred was close to retirement as the chairman of the US Postal Rate Commission, and as he listened to Chuck talk, he was profoundly touched. He believed that God was calling him to help, even if that meant doing so in a full-time capacity.

Chuck continued to study his Bible and read voraciously. He was especially impressed by Dietrich Bonhoeffer's *Letters and Papers from Prison*, which the German pastor and theologian had written during the two years he was imprisoned by the Nazis. This book began for Chuck a lifelong appreciation of Bonhoeffer and his writings. He realized that if Bonhoeffer hadn't been in prison, he never would have written those letters. This was part of how God showed Chuck that

"God causes all things to work together for good to those who love God, to those who are called according to His purpose" (Romans 8:28 NASB). Even prison.

◆ ◆ ◆

As January 1975 dawned, Chuck was filled with hope that he might be released early. Three other Watergate conspirators—John Dean, Jeb Magruder, and Herb Kalmbach—were being released early on the orders of US district judge John Sirica. But the gruff Judge Gerhard Gesell, who had jurisdiction over Chuck's case, did not feel inclined to follow Sirica's kindly lead. Colson, he decreed, would remain behind bars.

After having his and Patty's hopes raised so high by the release of the other three Watergate figures, the news came as a brutal blow. Life behind bars could be hard, even for someone filled with the peace, love, and joy of Jesus Christ, and it was agony to face the reality that he might have to spend another two years and five months in prison.

It was especially hard for Chuck, knowing that his innocent wife and children were suffering because of his misdeeds, forced to live their lives without him. The days following Gesell's decision were the toughest time of all for Chuck, and there was more bad news to come. On January 20, 1975, Chuck learned that the Virginia Supreme Court voted to disbar him from practicing law again. And there was still one more piece of bad news to come.

Chuck received word that his son Chris had been arrested for drug possession. To be unable to be there for his son at such an important time was heartbreaking. But this experience only deepened Chuck's empathy for his fellow prisoners, many of whom were going through similar situations. He took comfort in knowing that after he was released, he would remember the pain he was enduring now, and it would fire him up to help people facing similar trials.

On January 29, when Chuck was perhaps at his lowest ebb, his friend Harold Hughes came to visit. Chuck's four Fellowship friends had been regular visitors during his incarceration. But today Hughes saw that his friend had hit bottom. Hughes exhorted Chuck to practice what they all preached and to turn all his problems over to God. It sounded so simple, but doing it was not so easy. Nevertheless Chuck took his friend's advice, and that night in his cell, he prayed, giving everything to God. "Lord," he prayed,

> if this is what this is all about, then I thank you. I praise you for leaving me in prison, for letting them take away my license to practice law—yes, even for my son being arrested. I praise you for giving me your love through these men, for being God, for just letting me walk with Jesus.[16]

Somehow, that prayer changed everything; Chuck could feel it. Amidst his difficulties he experienced a joy that had been absent before. As Chuck recalled later, "This was the real mountaintop experience. Above and around me the world was filled with love and beauty. For the first time I felt truly free."[17]

What Chuck didn't know then was that outside the prison walls, his lawyer was talking to Judge Gesell again, asking whether he would at least give Chuck a ten-day furlough to be with his son, Chris, who badly needed his father. Gesell, who had been a hard-nosed and unpleasant judge and had proved he was not the sort to be budged, was somehow moved by all that he heard. He decided to rule in a way that no one could have anticipated. He wouldn't give Chuck a ten-day furlough. He decided to release Chuck permanently. In a moment, without a hint that this was a possibility, Chuck Colson was a free man. Was it a coincidence that after he had really turned everything over to God and felt truly free that this happened—that he was literally freed? Chuck didn't think so.

Not long afterward, Chuck arrived home to the same media glare he had left. He was disoriented by his sudden release, and whatever he managed to say was reduced to the following headline in the next day's *Washington Post*:

"Gesell Frees Colson. Colson Thanks the Lord."

Chuck's homecoming, with many friends and family there to greet him, was a warm one. Retiring to bed that night, he was alone with his thoughts for the first time in a long time. Finally falling asleep, he had a nightmare about being back at Maxwell. He dreamed that several prisoners were playing cards when one of them, a heavily tattooed six-foot-six inmate named Archie, menacingly confronted Chuck:

"You'll be out of here soon. What are you going to do for us?!"

Chuck somewhat lamely responded that he would help in some way.

"I'll never forget you guys, or this stinking place," he promised.

Archie wasn't buying it. He had heard promises like this before.

"There ain't nobody cares about us. Nobody!"

"I'll care," Chuck said. "I'll remember."[18]

Archie shouted back angrily with an expletive and underscored the word with an obscene gesture.

But Chuck's dream was not the product of his imagination; it was the memory of a real-life conversation with an inmate named Archie. The question was, why had he dreamed it? And what would he do about the promise he'd made?

His first priority had to be his family. Four days after arriving home, Chuck and Patty flew to visit Chris in Columbia, South Carolina. Instead of speaking sternly to his son, as he had planned, Chuck wrapped his arms around him and told him that everything would be all right. During their tearful reunion, Chuck realized that one of the most important things he would have to do, now that he was free and no longer had White House responsibilities, was to spend more time with his children, whom he had neglected during his rise to power.

After visiting Chris, Chuck flew to Maxwell Prison Camp for a reunion with old friends. That Chuck willingly entered the prison just a few days after he was released was a sign of things to come.

◆ ◆ ◆

With all that had happened and was still happening, Chuck and Patty badly needed to get away, so shortly after visiting Maxwell, they decided to fly to Spain for a real vacation. When they returned home, Chuck was still unclear about what to do next.

He couldn't practice law in Virginia, but there was a good possibility that he could do so in Massachusetts. He received lucrative business offers and endless speaking requests, many from Doug Coe and the brothers at the Fellowship. They wanted Chuck to speak publicly about how he came to faith in Jesus. But Chuck was still unsure of what he should be doing.

Then one day in April 1975, while staring at himself in the bathroom mirror, Chuck had a vision of what God wanted him to do with his life.

"As I stared at my reflection, a startling series of images flashed across my mind," Chuck later said.

> I saw men in prison gray moving about. Classes. Discussions. Prayers. The pictures became more sharply focused—of smiling men and women streaming out of prisons, of Bibles, and study groups around tables. These mental images lasted but a few seconds, then they were gone. I had never experienced anything like it before or since.[19]

Chuck was not the sort of Christian who would then or in the future talk much about mystical experiences. He was an extremely rational man. But he could not deny that this vision had occurred. What did it mean?

Then Chuck heard an almost audible voice, telling him, "Take the prisoners out, teach them, return them to prisons to build Christian fellowships. Spread these fellowships through every penitentiary in America."[20] Was he going crazy, or was God speaking to him?

Chuck immediately called his friend Harold Hughes. Surely Hughes would be able to make sense of it. Hughes drove over to Chuck's house, and they talked it over. Now the usually wide-eyed Hughes played the role of sober realist. There was no way to get prisoners out of prisons, he said.

But Chuck had never been one to let stubborn facts get in the way. He became convinced there was a way to turn this dream into a reality. After all, if God had given him this idea, surely God would find a way to achieve it, wouldn't he?

In June, Chuck and Harold met with the director of the Federal Bureau of Prisons, Norman Carlson. During their conversation, Carlson mentioned that he had been at a service in a California prison when a prisoner had prayed a spontaneous prayer for him and his wife. Why, Carlson asked Chuck, would that man pray for the very person who was keeping him behind bars?

"Mr. Carlson," Chuck replied, "that man prayed for you because he loves you."[21]

The answer clearly made an impression because Carlson unexpectedly told Chuck and Hughes that he would issue the order to bring Chuck's vision to America's prisons.

The Bureau of Prisons approved a proposal, brought to them by Chuck and Hughes, to allow the Fellowship Foundation to select federal prison inmates to attend a two-week retreat in the Washington DC area, at which the inmates would engage in Bible study and leadership training.

The results were exciting. Inmates from the first group offered to visit Arlington County Jail and Lorton Reformatory, both in Virginia, to talk to prisoners about God and his plan for their lives. After finishing their retreats, inmates returned to their prisons to begin prison fellowships—discipling their fellow inmates and finding ways to serve God behind bars. It worked, and it continued to work. The bold idea that God had given to Chuck Colson had become a reality.

As with everything that Chuck ever got involved with doing, he did it all the way. Within three years Prison Fellowship Ministries, as it was named, grew to employ one hundred employees in twenty-three states. Nearly seven thousand volunteers worked with inmates who had finished in-prison seminars in six hundred prisons. It was a remarkable achievement, making prison ministry a front-burner issue in many churches, many of which had forgotten that Jesus commands his followers to visit those in prison. Prison Fellowship International was also started, first in Great Britain and eventually in more than one hundred other countries.

◆ ◆ ◆

n 1976, Chuck wrote his first book, *Born Again*, which exploded onto the best-seller lists, and the term *born again* entered the popular lexicon as a description of someone who had a life-changing experience with God. Chuck soon made the commitment to devote himself full-time, for the rest of his life, to serving God in America's prisons. He also began deepening his knowledge of Christian teachings, meeting with Christian intellectuals and philosophers, such as Richard Mouw, Nicholas Wolterstorff, Stephen Monsma, R. C. Sproul, Dr. Carl Henry, Francis Schaeffer, Os Guinness, and Richard Lovelace. He read the writings of Luther, Zwingli, and Calvin, Abraham Kuyper, Paul Johnson, and fellow prisoners Alexander Solzhenitsyn and Dietrich Bonhoeffer. Chuck became convinced that it was absolutely necessary to develop a Christian worldview—a comprehensive framework regarding every aspect of life, from science to literature to film to politics.

One question that Chuck now explored was why people committed crimes in the first place. Some experts blamed poverty; others blamed race. But Chuck, studying the writings of sociologist James Q. Wilson, knew the real answer: crime is a moral problem that demands a moral solution. He was to hammer home this theme again and again. Commenting on a tragic school shooting in 1998, Chuck said:

What's happening to our children? The first thing we must understand is that only a biblical worldview of human nature can make
sense of these murders. The Bible makes two things clear about
humanity. First, we are created in the *imago Dei*, the image of God,
and knowledge of right and wrong is implanted on the human heart.
But we're also warned that we live in a fallen world—and that the
human heart is desperately wicked. These two facts require any
civilized society to make the moral training of its young its number
one priority. . . . The great criminologist James Q. Wilson says all
of his studies have led to the same conclusion: Crime begins when
children are not given adequate moral training, when they do not
develop internal restraints on impulsive behavior.[22]

Chuck's deep interest in worldview, and the need to teach it to
the faithful, resulted in the radio program *BreakPoint*, which rapidly grew until some eight million people were listening to it every
day. Later, wanting to influence the culture even more deeply, Chuck
established the Centurions Program, which accepts one hundred serious Christians each year into a yearlong distance-learning class in
which participants learn about worldviews—the Christian one and
those that compete against it—and develop a project in which to teach
what they've learned to their neighbors.

As the years passed, Chuck embraced other ways of ministering to
prisoners and their families. A former bank robber named Mary Kay
Beard convinced him to start a ministry called Angel Tree; ordinary
people purchase Christmas gifts for the children of prison inmates
and give them on behalf of a parent in prison who has no means of
giving gifts to his or her children personally.

In 1983, Chuck set up Justice Fellowship as a wing of Prison
Fellowship, devoted to criminal justice reform. He successfully fought
for a law that would do much to prevent prison rape. He fought for
the religious rights of prisoners—rights that were endangered by a
Supreme Court decision in the 1990s.

He wrote more books: *How Now Shall We Live?*, *Loving God*, *The Good Life*, *The Body*, *The Faith*, and many others.

In 1993, Chuck was awarded the one-million-dollar Templeton Prize for Progress in Religion. He donated the prize money to Prison Fellowship.

Each year, Chuck seemed to become busier and busier: magazine columns, speaking engagements, radio, prison visits, trips overseas to visit some of the most infamous gulags in the world.

Chuck so admired William Wilberforce that he set up the Wilberforce Award, given annually to a Christian who confronted social injustice, often related to human slavery. Winners include Philippine leader Benigno S. Aquino Jr., Bishop Macram Max Gassis, and Baroness Cox of Queensberry.

He also provoked intense controversy when he and Father Richard John Neuhaus set up a theological study group (and later wrote a document) they called "Evangelicals and Catholics Together"; its goal was to "minimize hostility and maximize cooperation between these two polarized pillars of the Christian world in the mission field." ECT also attempted to reconcile theological differences between the two groups.

In 1999, with the help of then Governor George W. Bush, Prison Fellowship took over a wing of a Texas prison for the InnerChange Freedom Initiative, a program in which prisoners volunteer for a tough, Bible-based program of activities that prepare them for successful reentry into society when they finish their sentences.

Chuck constantly fought the culture of death, especially when his friend President George W. Bush was in the White House, encouraging the president, with considerable success, to get behind efforts to fight human trafficking, end the civil war in Sudan, combat the global spread of AIDS, and protect persecuted Christians in the Middle East. In the process, Chuck helped to change the image of Christianity in the minds of many secular observers, earning the admiration of those who had previously disdained what Christians stood for.

Chuck's biggest fault, as those who knew him will attest, was that he was always trying to do too much. In the last two or three years of his life, this human tornado seemed to be conscious that time was running out for him. His two last big projects began in 2009, when he was seventy-seven years old. The first was establishing the Chuck Colson Center for Christian Worldview, which promotes worldview teaching, and the second was helping write the Manhattan Declaration, which calls for the church to defend the sanctity of human life, traditional marriage, and freedom of religion.

In the weeks before his death at age eighty, Chuck was planning yet another big project, "perhaps the biggest of all," writes former *BreakPoint* managing editor James Tonkowich. "A movement of Christians to reform education—public, charter, private and Christian—from Kindergarten through university. This is a vast undertaking for someone half his age, but then again, [Chuck] never thought that way."[23]

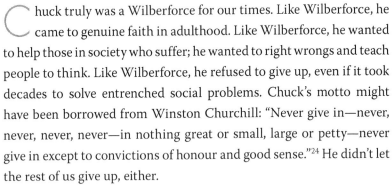

Chuck truly was a Wilberforce for our times. Like Wilberforce, he came to genuine faith in adulthood. Like Wilberforce, he wanted to help those in society who suffer; he wanted to right wrongs and teach people to think. Like Wilberforce, he refused to give up, even if it took decades to solve entrenched social problems. Chuck's motto might have been borrowed from Winston Churchill: "Never give in—never, never, never, never—in nothing great or small, large or petty—never give in except to convictions of honour and good sense."[24] He didn't let the rest of us give up, either.

Throughout his ministry, Chuck loved to say that no matter what, Christians must be at their posts, doing their duty. And that message—stay at your posts—was on the pins that mourners were given at the Washington National Cathedral memorial service, attended by the great and the powerful of the land, who sat side by side with those who, like Chuck, had once been locked away behind bars. People Chuck had loved and served, dined with and prayed with.

Chuck's message to stay at your posts was echoed by his daughter, Emily, who told mourners,

> Today is a celebration of my father's life, but today is also about us—you and me. What will we do in the shadow of such an extraordinary role model?
>
> There is work to be done. I encourage you to continue the work God has begun through my father's life. Do the right thing, seek the truth, defend the weak, live courageous lives.[25]

Chuck's last words to us, which he left with his family, were a final witness to the God he served. "I want my funeral services to be joyful," he wrote. "I don't want people to be sad because I believe with every ounce of conviction in my body that death is but a homecoming, and that we'll be in the presence of God. It's the culmination of life. It's a celebration."[26]

Do you believe that? It's true.

Acknowledgments

Previously, whenever someone asked me who helped research my books—especially the Wilberforce and Bonhoeffer biographies—I usually laughed, saying how much I wished that had been possible, but making clear that no one had helped, that I had done every jot of research and had written every tittle myself. My process was something like juggling while riding a unicycle. One did it alone or one didn't do it at all. This book, however, happily marks at least a one-volume departure from the standard juggling and unicycling. For the first time I am happy to have had help, most notably from my friend Anne Morse—especially on the Washington, Liddell, and Robinson chapters—and from our *BreakPoint* colleague Gina Dalfonzo, who helped with the Wojtyla chapter. I also must here acknowledge another *BreakPoint* colleague, my dear friend Roberto Rivera, who in 1998 tipped me off to Jackie Robinson's faith—and Branch Rickey's—and alerted me to the definitive Arnold Rampersad biography. Finally, I wish to acknowledge and thank my dear friend Markus Spieker, whose encouragement to write a book along these lines has finally borne fruit. May it continue to do so.

— Eric Metaxas
New York City
November 2012

Notes

CHAPTER 1: GEORGE WASHINGTON

1. Henry Wiencek, *An Imperfect God: George Washington, His Slaves, and the Creation of America* (Reprint, New York: Farrar, Straus and Giroux, 2004), 46.
2. John Ferling, *The Ascent of George Washington* (New York: Bloomsbury Press, 2010), 10.
3. Ibid.
4. Ibid., 10–11.
5. Ibid., 13.
6. Ibid., 16.
7. Edward G. Lengel, *General George Washington: A Military Life* (New York: Random House Trade Paperbacks, 2007), 35.
8. Ferling, *The Ascent of George Washington*, 21.
9. Ron Chernow, *Washington: A Life* (New York: The Penguin Press, 2010), 42.
10. Ferling, *The Ascent of George Washington*, 21.
11. Ibid., 22.
12. Ibid., 24.
13. Chernow, *Washington: A Life*, 42.
14. Ibid., 50.
15. Ferling, *The Ascent of George Washington*, 29.
16. Ibid.
17. Chernow, *Washington: A Life*, 92.
18. Ferling, *The Ascent of George Washington*, 75.

19. David A. Adler, *George Washington: An Illustrated Biography* (New York: Holiday House, 2004), 94.

20. *The Papers of George Washington*, accessed November 26, 2012, http://gwpapers.virginia.edu/documents/revolution/letters/gfairfax2.html.

21. "Battle of Bunker Hill" http://en.wikipedia.org/wiki/Battle_of_Bunker_Hill.

22. Chernow, *Washington: A Life*, 186.

23. Ibid., 187.

24. Ibid., 189.

25. Adler, *George Washington: An Illustrated Biography*, 149.

26. Chernow, *Washington: A Life*, 133.

27. Ibid., 132.

28. Ibid., 131.

29. Ibid., 133.

30. Ibid.

31. "Washington's Farewell Address, 1976," accessed November 26, 2012, http://avalon.law.yale.edu/18th_century/washing.asp.

32. Adler, *George Washington: An Illustrated Biography*, 150.

33. Ibid., 152.

34. Joseph J. Ellis, *His Excellency George Washington* (London: Vintage, 2005), 139.

35. Ibid., 141.

36. Ferling, *The Ascent of George Washington*, 232.

37. Ellis, *His Excellency George Washington*, 142.

38. "George Washington Prevents the Revolt of his Officers," accessed November 26, 2012, http://www.historyplace.com/speeches/washington.htm.

39. Ibid.

40. Ibid.

41. Ibid.

42. Ibid.

43. Ibid.

44. Ibid.

45. Chernow, *Washington: A Life*, 435–436.

46. Ellis, *His Excellency George Washington*, 141.

47. Ibid., 139.

48. "The American Revolution, 1763–1783," accessed November 26, 2012, http://www.loc.gov/teachers/classroommaterials/presentationsandactivities/presentations/timeline/amrev/contarmy/newyork.html.

49. Ellis, *His Excellency George Washington*, 274–275.

50. Ferling, *The Ascent of George Washington*, 306.

51. Ibid.

52. "The American Revolution, 1763–1783," accessed November 26, 2012, http://www.loc.gov/teachers/classroommaterials/presentationsandactivities/presentations/timeline/amrev/contarmy/newyork.html.

53. George Washington, *Washington on Washington* (Lexington, KY: The University Press of Kentucky, 2003), 138.

54. Ellis, *His Excellency George Washington*, 268.

55. Barnes Historical Series, *A Brief History of the United States* (Whitefish, MT: Kessinger Publishing, 2004), 101.

56. Ferling, *The Ascent of George Washington*, 370–371.

57. Ellis, *His Excellency George Washington*, 270.

58. Ibid., 270–271.

59. Adler, *George Washington: An Illustrated Biography*, 206.

CHAPTER 2: WILLIAM WILBERFORCE

1. Isaiah 61:1, Luke 4:18 NKJV.

2. Robert Isaac Wilberforce and Samuel Wilberforce, *The Life of William Wilberforce*, vol. 4 (London: John Murray, 1838), 373.

3. *Joni Eareckson Tada 2012 Wilberforce Award Recipient*, http://www .breakpoint.org/wilberforce-weekend-2012/wilberforce-award.

4. Robert Isaac Wilberforce and Samuel Wilberforce, *The Life of William Wilberforce*, vol. 1 (London: John Murray, 1838), 7.

5. Ibid.

6. Earl Philip Henry Stanhope, *Life of the Right Honourable William Pitt*, vol. 1, (London: John Murray, 1862), 283.

7. E. M. Forster, *Marianne Thornton: A Domestic Biography* (London: Hodder and Stoughton, 1956), 43.

8. Wilberforce and Wilberforce, *The Life of William Wilberforce*, vol. 1, 75.

9. Ibid.

10. John S. Harford, *Recollections of William Wilberforce During Nearly Thirty Years* (London: Longman, Green, Longman, Roberts and Green, 1864), 216.

11. William Wilberforce, "Journal, Sunday, October 28, 1787," quoted in Wilberforce and Wilberforce, *The Life of William Wilberforce*, vol. 1, 149.

12. Wilfrid Prest, *Albion Ascendant: English History, 1660–1815* (Oxford: Oxford University Press, 1998).

13. John Wesley, "Letter to William Wilberforce, London, February 24, 1791," in Thomas Jackson, ed., *The Works of John Wesley*, 14 vols. (Franklin, TN: Providence House, 1994), CD-ROM, 13:153.

14. John Charles Pollock, *Wilberforce* (London: Constable, 1977), 64.

15. William Wilberforce, in "Debate on Mr. Wilberforce's Resolutions respecting the Slave Trade," in William Cobbett, *The Parliamentary History of England. From the Norman Conquest in 1066 to the year 1803*, vol. 28 (1789–91), (London: T. Curson Hansard, 1806–1820), cols 42–68.

CHAPTER 3: ERIC LIDDELL

1. *Eric Liddell: Champion of Conviction* (Dolby DVD, January 2008).

2. Catherine Swift, *Eric Liddell* (Ada, MI: Bethany House Publishers, 1990), 78.

3. *Eric Liddell: Champion of Conviction*.

4. Ibid.

5. RBC Ministries, *Our Daily Bread*, "Life-Changing Choices," accessed January 17, 2013, http://mobi.rbc.org/odb/2012-08-04.html.

6. David Brooks, "The Jeremy Lin Problem," *New York Times*, February 16, 2012, http://www.nytimes.com/2012/02/17 /opinion/brooks-the-jeremy-lin-problem.html.

7. Swift, *Eric Liddell*, 86.

8. David McCasland, *Eric Liddell: Pure Gold* (Grand Rapids, MI: Discovery House Publishers, 2001), 80.

9. C. S. Lewis Institute, Joel S. Woodruff, Ed.D., "Eric Liddell: Muscular Discipline and Olympic Champion," Summer 2012, http://www .cslewisinstitute.org/webfm_send/1386.

10. McCasland, *Eric Liddell: Pure Gold*, 103.

11. Ibid., 96.

12. http://en.wikipedia.org/wiki/Horatio_Fitch.

13. McCasland, *Eric Liddell: Pure Gold*, 98.

14. Ibid., 101.

15. *Eric Liddell: Champion of Conviction.*

16. Hugh Hudson, *Chariots of Fire* (Dolby DVD, January 2004).

17. McCasland, *Eric Liddell: Pure Gold*, 210.

18. Ibid., 223.

19. Ibid.

20. Eric Liddell, *Disciplines of the Christian Life* (eChristian Books, Kindle Edition, January 2011).

21. *Eric Liddell: Champion of Conviction.*

22. McCasland, *Eric Liddell: Pure Gold*, 268.

23. Ibid., 269.

24. *Eric Liddell: Champion of Conviction.*

25. McCasland, *Eric Liddell: Pure Gold*, 279.

26. Ibid., 280.

27. *Eric Liddell: Champion of Conviction.*

28. Ibid.

29. Ibid.

30. Ibid.

31. *From the Ends of the Earth*, "Marinating in the Word," June 17, 2012, http://bencarswell.blogspot.com/2012/06/marinating-in-word.html.

32. BBC, "Golden Scots," June 25, 2012, http://www .bbc.co.uk/sport/0/scotland/18534527.

33. McCasland, *Eric Liddell: Pure Gold*, 105.

34. James H. Taylor, III, Weihsien Paintings, accessed January 10, 2013, http:// www.weihsien-paintings.org/NormanCliff/people/individuals/Eric01 /PureGold/txt_foreword.htm.

CHAPTER 4: DIETRICH BONHOEFFER

1. Liebholz-Bonhoeffer, Sabine, *The Bonhoeffers: Portrait of a Family* (New York: St. Martin's, 1971), 21–22.
2. James 1:12 ESV.
3. "Inge Karding interviewed by Martin Doblmeier," *Bonhoeffer*, directed by Martin Doblmeier (First Run Features, 2003), DVD.
4. This statement has been "traced to 1933, though never recorded in writing" according to Stephen R. Haynes, *The Bonhoeffer Legacy: Post-Holocaust Perspectives* (Minneapolis: Fortress Press, 2006), 32–33.
5. "Outline for a Book," August 8, 1944, in John W. De Gruchy, ed., *Letters and Papers from Prison*, vol. 8, *Dietrich Bonhoeffer Works* (Minneapolis: Augsburg Fortress, 2010), 501.
6. The famous "First they came . . ." statement by Martin Niemöller was delivered in diverse variations during his many postwar speaking engagements. This most definitive version was published by Franklin Littell, who knew Niemöller. Franklin H. Littell, "First They Came for the Jews," *Christian Ethics Today* issue 9, vol. 3, no. 1 (February 1997), 29.
7. Wolf-Dieter Zimmermann and Ronald G. Smith, eds., *I Knew Dietrich Bonhoeffer*, Käthe G. Smith, trans, (New York: Harper and Row, 1966), 158–160.
8. Michael Robert Marrus, *The Nazi Holocaust. Part 8: Bystanders to the Holocaust*, vol. 1 (Munich: KG Saur Verlag, 1989), 1401, citing Eberhard Bethge, *Dietrich Bonhoeffer: A Biography*, Victoria J. Barnett, ed. (Minneapolis: Fortress, 1967–2000).
9. Keith Clements, ed., *London: 1933–1935*, vol. 13, *Dietrich Bonhoeffer Work* (New York: Fortress, 2007), 331.
10. John W. De Gruchy, ed., *Letters and Papers from Prison*, vol. 8, *Dietrich Bonhoeffer Works* (Minneapolis: Augsburg Fortress, 2010), 370–372.
11. Dietrich Bonhoeffer, *The Cost of Discipleship* (London: SCM, 1959), 99.

CHAPTER 5: JACKIE ROBINSON

1. Arnold Rampersad, *Jackie Robinson* (New York: Ballantine Books, 1998), 24.
2. Ibid., 51.
3. Ibid., 96.
4. Scott Simon, *Jackie Robinson and the Integration of Baseball* (Hoboken, NJ: John Wiley & Sons, Inc., 2007), 19.
5. Rampersad, *Jackie Robinson*, 103.
6. Ibid., 106.
7. Ibid.
8. Ibid., 107.
9. Ibid., 122.
10. Simon, *Jackie Robinson and the Integration of Baseball*, 63.
11. Rampersad, *Jackie Robinson*, 125.
12. Ibid., 126.

13. Ibid., 127.

14. Ibid., 129.

15. Murrey Polner, *Branch Rickey, A Biography* (Jefferson, NC: McFarland & Company, 2007), 176.

16. Jackie Robinson, Alfred Duckett, *I Never Had It Made: An Autobiography of Jackie Robinson* (New York: Harper Perennial, 2003), 41.

17. Rampersad, *Jackie Robinson*, 167.

18. Robinson, Duckett, *I Never Had It Made*, 58.

19. Rampersad, *Jackie Robinson*, 173.

20. Simon, *Jackie Robinson and the Integration of Baseball*, 122.

21. Jonathan Eig, *Opening Day: The Story of Jackie Robinson's First Season* (New York: Simon & Schuster, 2007), 224.

22. Sharon Robinson, *Jackie's Nine: Jackie Robinson's Values to Live By* (New York: Scholastic Inc., 2002), 89.

23. Rachel Robinson, *Jackie Robinson: An Intimate Portrait* (New York: Abradale /Abrams, 1998), 216.

24. ESPN's 100 Most Memorable Moments, "93: Baseball retires Jackie Robinson's No. 42," accessed November 26, 2012, http://sports.espn.go.com/espn/espn25 /story?page=moments/93.

CHAPTER 6: POPE JOHN PAUL II

1. Monsignor Virgilio Levi and Christine Allison, *John Paul II: A Tribute in Words and Pictures* (New York: William Morrow & Company, 1999).

2. David Aikman, *Great Souls: Six Who Changed a Century* (Lanham, MD: Lexington Books, 2003), 272.

3. George Weigel, *Witness to Hope* (New York: HarperCollins, 2001), 56–57.

4. Aikman, *Great Souls: Six Who Changed a Century*, 277.

5. Weigel, *Witness to Hope*, 57.

6. Ibid., 68.

7. Aikman, *Great Souls: Six Who Changed a Century*, 283.

8. Ibid., 285.

9. Weigel, *Witness to Hope*, 142.

10. Ibid., 164.

11. Aikman, *Great Souls: Six Who Changed a Century*, 296.

12. Weigel, *Witness to Hope*, 254.

13. Gunther Simmermacher, "The Southern Cross," October 15–21, 2003, http://www.mail-archive.com/pope-john-paul-ii@yahoogroups.com/msg00008.html.

14. Aikman, *Great Souls: Six Who Changed a Century*, 253.

15. Ibid., 262.

16. Ibid., 255.

17. Monsignor Virgilio Levi and Christine Allison, *John Paul II: A Tribute in Words and Pictures*, 113–116.

18. Stanislaw Dziwisz, *A Life with Karol: My Forty-Year Friendship with the Man Who Became Pope* (New York: Doubleday, 2008), 237.

19. Levi and Allison, *John Paul II: A Tribute in Words and Pictures*, 116.

20. Dziwisz, *A Life with Karol*, 249.

21. Aikman, *Great Souls: Six Who Changed a Century*, 301–2.

22. CNN World, "Vatican Reasserts Stem Cell Stand," CNN.com, July 25, 2001.

23. George Weigel, *The End and the Beginning: Pope John Paul II—The Victory of Freedom, the Last Years, the Legacy* (New York: Image, 2011), 370–371.

24. Ibid., 385.

25. Ibid., 418.

26. Ibid., 429.

27. Aikman, *Great Souls: Six Who Changed a Century*, 307.

CHAPTER 7: CHARLES W. COLSON

1. Charles W. Colson, *Born Again* (Ada, MI: Chosen Books, 1976), 24.

2. Ibid., 26–27.

3. Jonathan Aitken, *Charles W. Colson: A Life Redeemed* (Colorado Springs, CO: Waterbrook Press, 2005), 194.

4. Colson, *Born Again*, 109.

5. Psalm 37:1, 3–5 NIV.

6. Colson, *Born Again*, 115–116.

7. Ibid., 117.

8. Ibid.

9. Ibid., 125.

10. Aitken, *Charles W. Colson: A Life Redeemed*, 220.

11. Colson, *Born Again*, 150.

12. Aitken, *Charles W. Colson: A Life Redeemed*, 241.

13. Ibid., 248.

14. Ibid., 254–255.

15. Ibid., 258.

16. Ibid., 278.

17. Ibid.

18. Ibid., 271.

19. Ibid., 274.

20. Ibid., 276.

21. Ibid.

22. Chuck Colson, "Kids Who Kill," BreakPoint.org, March 30, 1998.

23. Jim Tonkowich, "The Wideness of Worldview: Remembering Chuck Colson," April 23, 2012, http://www.religiontoday.com/news/wideness-of-worldview-remembering-chuck-colson.html.

24. Winston Churchill, speech at Harrow School, October 29, 1941, http://www.winstonchurchill.org/learn/speeches/speeches-of-winston-churchill/103-never-give-in.

25. As remembered by the author.

26. Ibid.

Index

About the Author

Eric Metaxas is the author of *New York Times* #1 bestseller and ECPA "Book of the Year" *Bonhoeffer: Pastor, Martyr, Prophet, Spy,* the bestseller *Amazing Grace: William Wilberforce and the Heroic Campaign to End Slavery,* and more than thirty other books. He is currently the voice of *BreakPoint,* a radio commentary broadcast on fourteen hundred radio outlets with an audience of 8 million. Metaxas was the keynote speaker at the 2012 National Prayer Breakfast in Washington, DC, and was awarded the Canterbury Medal in 2011 by the Becket Fund for Religious Freedom. Metaxas has written for VeggieTales, Chuck Colson, and the *New York Times.* He currently lives in New York with his wife and daughter.